Jo Draper is an archaeolo͵
editor of the *Proceedings of the Dorset Natural History &
Archaeological Society* for fifteen years. She has written
several books on the county including *Dorset, The Complete Guide.* Christopher Chaplin is a land surveyor and
archaeologist, and is the author of *Dorset from the Air.*
They live in Dorchester, and have enjoyed walking in
Dorset for more than 25 years.

Following page
St Catherine's Chapel, Abbotsbury.
[see Walk 6]

Walking DORSET HISTORY

Jo Draper & Christopher Chaplin

Line drawings by Dennis Burden

THE DOVECOTE PRESS

For Richard and Karin
who enjoy Dorset walking

First published in 1997 by the Dovecote Press Ltd
Stanbridge, Wimborne, Dorset BH21 4JD

ISBN 1 874336 37 7

© Jo Draper & Christopher Chaplin 1997
© Line drawings, Dennis Burden 1997

Phototypeset by the Typesetting Bureau
Wimborne, Dorset
Printed and bound by Biddles Ltd
Guildford and King's Lynn

1 3 5 7 9 8 6 4 2

Contents

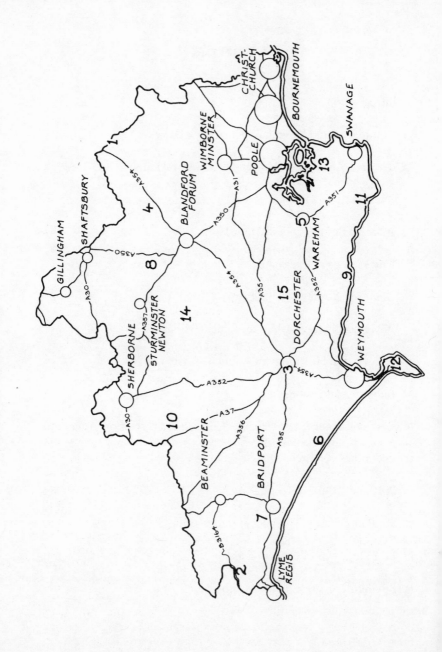

Introduction

The famous and well-loved landscapes of Dorset are full of their own history. They were first created by their geology, and by the natural vegetation, but for at least five thousand years they have been adapted by the people who have lived here.

The great variety of countryside within the county has been produced by the very diverse geology - most of the geological strata of England are to be found in Dorset. The boldest contrasts and most dramatic landscapes are along the coast, but there is much variation inland from the rather domestic, well-hedged clay vales, through the high and open chalk hills, to the wild, uncultivated (but sadly shrinking) heathlands.

Man has steadily adapted his habitat, and virtually all the vegetation has been changed from its original form, mostly for farming but also for quarrying and so on. We shall explore the effects of man on the landscape from prehistoric times up to the early 20th century, tracing the features in the landscape which show its past. On foot is the finest way to see any landscape: the pace is slow enough to take in all the details, but fast enough to see a decent area.

The walks range from the spectacular Purbeck coastline to lesser-known areas inland, taking in the chalk downs, the heathlands, the clay vales and two of the historic towns.

Each of these fifteen walks is centred around a particular part of Dorset's history and has also been designed to make a good walk. We have tried to route them off the roads wherever possible, and through the best landscapes with the greatest variety of vegetation. They are all circular, and the longer ones have short-cuts offered for those who do not want to walk too far. Advice on parking and public transport is given for each one, and information on pubs, cafes, lavatories etc, close to, or on, the route. The introduction to each specifies the length, any steep slopes and the general nature of the walk.

Season and weather made a great difference. We walked most of these routes in a flaming hot summer (and more suitably in the subsequent glorious autumn), and saw the Blackmore Vale at its driest for years, with the pastures everywhere steadily turning brown. All the walks were dryer then than they usually are, but all should be possible throughout the year. Boots or strong shoes are recommended for all of them at all seasons. In winter wellingtons would be better for those off the quick-drying chalk. We have seen clouds of butterflies, occasional deer, foxes and lots of birds and rabbits, besides many varieties of wild flowers.

The maps are all at the same scale (except the two town maps for Dorchester and Wareham, and the one for Walk 10), so comparison is easy. The map and text are linked by spots marked A,B,C etc. Short-cut routes are placed in square brackets.

The details given in the text and maps were correct at the time of writing, but the countryside is always changing and even in the short period between our walking one and the 'tester' doing so, one walk altered a tiny bit and one part of Purbeck, seemingly unchanged for fifty years, suddenly developed a long new track. We have tried to indicate the general direction of the walk so that minor changes won't leave you lost.

Footpaths are rights of way: everyone has the right to walk along them, but all walkers should behave responsibly. If you open a gate, please be sure to close it after you. Dogs should be kept on their leads to ensure that they do not disturb livestock. One must respect the countryside, protect wildlife and not interfere with farming.

We have walked all these routes, and then they have been checked by kind friends who have walked them with the maps and instructions. We are very grateful to Peter Bellamy; Alicia and Peter Bentley; Richard and Karin Coode; Mike King; Shirley and George Wickham; and Tracey Hewitt for trying out the walks, and for their comments. They are not responsible for any remaining errors: the authors are.

We are grateful to Theresa Hall, Lilian Ladle and Dr Peter Stanier for answering queries, and to Marion Makinson for reading the whole text and for her comments. Sheena Pearce has typed everything for us quickly, cheerfully and accurately, as usual. The Dorset County Library has yet again willingly found us obscure books, articles, prints, and maps. The County Surveyor's Department, County Hall, Dorchester helped us with several queries. Many thanks.

Boundaries and Downland – Bokerley Dyke

This walk traces one of the best earthworks in the county, and is within a huge area of original downland, a Nature Reserve particularly noted for its downland flora, birds and butterflies. The main route is 5 miles (8km) virtually all on downland, and involves climbing 450ft (140m). The shortened route is 2 miles (3km). The paths are well-marked, easy to find and virtually all on turf.

Introduction: Bokerley Dyke marks the boundary between Dorset and Hampshire, and parts of the walk are in the latter county. The area also has an earlier earthern boundary – Grim's Ditch, suggesting that this ridge has formed the junction of two different regions for a very long time. The dykes and Roman road are the biggest and clearest parts of a complicated series of earthworks and crop marks spreading over a huge area and ranging in date from the Neolithic (5,000 years ago) to medieval times.

Parking and Public Transport: Drive to Martin (Hampshire) and follow the lane (Sillens Lane) which turns west where there is a little triangular green in the middle of the village. After ³/4 mile this terminates at the car park for Martin Down Nature Reserve (A on the map SU057191). The Weymouth-Salisbury buses go along the main road, and can be taken from Blandford too.

Information: No cafes, pubs or lavatories on the whole of this walk, except occasionally a van in the layby near E.

Directions:
Facing the Nature Reserve, with the chalk hills beyond, take the gravel track on the left, or the path in the grass parallel with it. An overgrown hedge on the left marks the boundary of the Nature Reserve. Continue along this track, ignoring left turn to Downs Farm. After a dip ignore the branch to the right and continue up the track which turns left. Although mostly in Hampshire, this vast area of downland gives a good idea of what the chalklands of Dorset looked like before they were enclosed and ploughed. Smooth rolling hills, with no fences, covered with downland turf. Travellers through Dorset often commented on the bleak chalk uplands, which had no villages and were only peopled by a few shepherds and many sheep. Even the roads were unfenced, producing a bare countryside

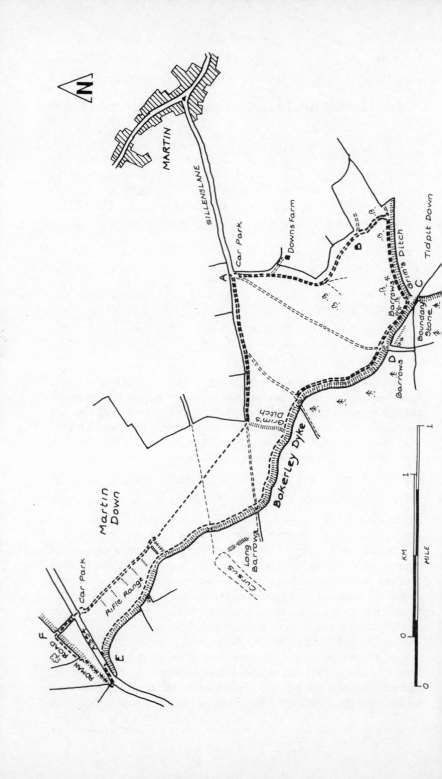

which few admired. *At the base of the steep slope* (B) *take the right hand track up the slope, with scrub on both sides. At the top of the hill follow the track round the bend to the right.*

Just round the corner, on the top of the hill, are a bank and ditch, with the bank about 2m high from the base of the ditch. This is Grim's Ditch, part of the complex of earthworks spread over this whole area. Grim's Ditch is probably Bronze Age (3,500 years ago), a well-preserved example of a type of boundary found all over Hampshire, Wiltshire and Dorset. Usually the bank has been ploughed away, with the ditch only showing as a crop-mark on aerial photos.

Follow along Grim's Ditch until it joins a larger bank and ditch (C), Bokerley Dyke, the largest surviving earthwork in the area. The impressive bank with ditch in front runs for nearly 4 miles, and is defending the area which is now Dorset. It runs between two areas of woodland on clay soil, protecting the open chalklands which would have been easy for armies on foot to move across. The woodlands would have impeded their advance. The bank was nearly 3m (9ft) high and the ditch 3m (9ft) deep, and at maximum the defences were 35m (100ft) across. Silting and erosion over the years has filled part of the ditch. The gap here may be an original entrance. Part of the dyke to the left has recently been cleared of trees, and has a boundary stone of 1891, presumably marking the Cranborne estate of the Marquis of Salisbury. A small bank inside the wood is part of a medieval deer park, mentioned in 1321. The deer park used Bokerley Dyke for another of its boundaries. Old trees on the dyke here.

Continue on the track down the hill beside Bokerley Dyke, which forms the boundary between Hampshire and Dorset for its whole length. To walk in Dorset stay on top of the bank which can be rough walking. On the right are two Bronze Age round barrows, both showing central depressions left by Sir Richard Colt-Hoare when he dug into them in 1805. He found burial urns in both.

The date of Bokerley Dyke depends on evidence from excavations, most of which have been at the northern end, by the Roman road (see later in the walk) and by its placing in relationship to other earthworks. The siting of the barrows here and a little further on, neatly close to the dyke, could suggest that they are contemporary, and that the earliest version of Bokerley is Bronze Age.

Another, straighter ditch and bank can be seen inside (the Dorset side of) Bokerley Dyke, with two more barrows just beyond it. The bank and ditch continue in an almost straight line almost to the Roman road, and are generally considered to be earlier than Bokerley Dyke itself, although it has recently been suggested that they

A view of Bokerley Dyke

could be contemporary, as bends in the smaller bank correspond to changes in angle of Bokerley Dyke.

The gap through the Dyke here is for the old Cranborne Road, and may be medieval. Walk up the path though for a better view of the barrows.

[To shorten the walk take the track leading right here (D), which will lead back to the car park. Drive north through Martin, and back west along the main road and park in the car park signed just before Bokerley Dyke to rejoin the last part of the walk].

Continue along the track beside Bokerley Dyke (or on top of it). After a small rise another ditch and bank is seen at right angles to Bokerley. Part of the continuation of this earthwork was excavated, in the 1880s, and proved to be Bronze Age.

Keep on the track, and in the ploughed field to the left two Neolithic long barrows can be seen, one particularly clearly because it has trees on. Both are close to the end of the ploughed-out Dorset Cursus, a strange Neolithic earthwork of two banks 100-120m (3-400ft) apart, which runs for 6¼ miles across the chalk downland, starting here. Its purpose is not known, but it is difficult to see how it could have been useful, so presumably it had religious significance. The long barrows and cursus are the earliest monuments in this area, certainly pre-dating the dykes.

Continue along parallel with (or on) the bank. On the right is a 19th-century rifle range, with banks around. Here Bokerley has been partly dug away, probably for chalk to lime the fields, in the 19th century.

At the next bend there is a short extension to the Dyke, a length of bank and ditch added at right angles to the main bank. This may be a Roman addition.

Further along the dyke there are many rabbit burrows – they prefer the slightly softer chalk of the bank. Bokerley Dyke turns inwards. *Continue along it, pass through the metal gate onto the main road* (E), *cross to the small lay-by car park.* The modern road uses the ancient gap in the dyke, but is on a slightly different line in Dorset, and a very different one in Hampshire from the Roman one. Bokerley Dyke is the most damaged here – road widening here in the 1880s produced Roman coins, which is why the local pioneer archaeologist Pitt-Rivers decided to excavate in the late 19th century. A Second World War searchlight post was constructed on the south side of the road. The density of earthworks and settlements in this area (mostly damaged by ploughing) is complex, but basically Pitt-Rivers demonstrated that this part of Bokerley was built (or possibly rebuilt) in the late Roman period. An Iron Age and Roman settlement on the north side of the road is largely ploughed out, but shows as crop marks. A defensive earthwork here in the 5th century, at the end of the Roman period, would have been constructed to prevent the invading Saxons taking over Dorset. Early Saxon settlements and burials are found east of Bokerley in Wiltshire and Hampshire, but not in Dorset, so the Saxons were successfully kept out in the 5th and 6th centuries AD. This is the time of the legendary King Arthur, the British hero who repulsed the Saxons. The Saxons spread into Dorset from the end of the 7th century.

George Lipscombe, one of the many travellers along the main road, asked shepherds here in 1799 where Bokerley Dyke terminated. One suggested 'a terrible ways off' and another 'they zays it goes to Vrance, but I never zeed it myself'.

Straight on across the car park, following the path directly right (marked Bridleway) which runs along the prominent hump in the field. This is the Roman road, still showing clearly despite having been quarried in the mid 19th century to provide gravel for the modern road. The Roman road changes angle at Bokerley Dyke, which could suggest that the dyke was there first. Good view back over Bokerley Dyke. The Roman road ahead is used as the boundary between Wiltshire and Hampshire.

Take the track leading right (F) *back to the main road, cross the road and go through the car park, bearing right on the main gravelled track which leads through scrub and out into open grassland.* The rifle ranges are on the right.

The Nature Reserve is one of the few large areas of flat downland to survive. Parts were ploughed during the Second World War, but they are gradually reverting to the natural grassland. Areas are temporarily fenced off to protect nesting birds, or for sheep. The grass must be grazed: if left it would all revert to scrub.

Ignore right or left turns. One of the banks seen earlier is on the right. *Keep on along the edge of the reserve on the clear track, and the car park comes into view.*

The Iron Age in West Dorset
Coney's and Lambert's Castles

A short (4 miles, 6½km) walk around two hillforts, with one steady ascent which takes up most of the 500ft (150m) climbing. Well-marked paths, many thick hedgerows and panoramic views. Parts of the track through Higher Coombe can be muddy.

Lambert's and Coney's are two of the smaller Iron Age hillforts of Dorset and are surprisingly close together. In the Iron Age (600 BC to 43 AD) they were on the boundary between two tribes, and they are close to the modern county boundary between Dorset and Devon.

Parking: The hillforts are in an obscure part of the Marshwood Vale, and can be reached from Charmouth or Morcombelake on the A35, by those who are very good at navigation using the Ordnance Survey maps. Neither are signposted at all, and it is easier to find them from the north or west. Approaching from the north, take the B3165 to Marshwood and keep straight on through the sparse village. On the western outskirts you will find the Bottle Inn (right). A quarter of a mile west along the road from the inn, take the first left, which is not signposted at all. Keep on along this road for 3/4 mile until you reach a junction where five minor roads meet (point D on the map). See end of paragraph to reach the car-park. Another route is to take the A35 west after the Lyme Regis turn-off for 2 miles and then right onto the B3165 (signposted Marshwood, Crewkerne) for 3 miles. Turn right (signposted Fishpond) downhill for ½ mile to the junction of five minor roads (point D on the map). Once you have reached point D, (from whichever direction you have approached it), take the road southwards and uphill signed Wooton Fitzpaine and after ¼ mile, at the top of the hill, on the left, is the National Trust car-park (A on the map SY371977). The area is not accessible by public transport.

Information: No lavatories or cafes on the route. Many can be found in Charmouth, on the coast 2½ miles (4km) to the south. The nearest pub is at Marshwood, ½ mile (1km) north-east of Lambert's Castle.

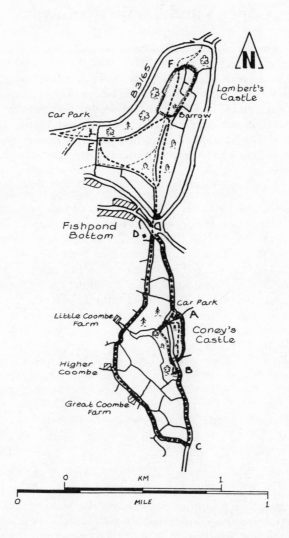

N

B3165

F

Lambert's
Castle

Car Park

Barrow

E

Fishpond
Bottom

D

Car Park

Little Coombe
Farm

A

Coney's
Castle

Higher
Coombe

B

Great Coombe
Farm

C

0	KM	1
0	MILE	1

Directions:

Go to the footpath marked 'Entrance' leading directly out of the car park. Don't follow sign to entrance, but turn left along the central ditch between the two ramparts. A clear path leads along the ditch right round the defences. At the first corner a modern field bank fills the ditch. Go over its bank, sharp right and down over into the Iron Age ditch. Coney's Castle is small, but the defences are impressive, running around the end of the spur of the hill, which is 702ft (214m) high. The many hillforts in Dorset, all with earthen defences, suggest that war was not uncommon in the Iron Age. It used to be thought that hillforts were refuges, only used in times of war, but where excavated they have proved to have been permanently occupied. Coney's is simple compared to large developed hillforts like Maiden Castle (or Hambledon Hill – see Walk 8), and probably dates from early on in the Iron Age. The name suggests that the castle is called Rabbit's Castle (Coney is the old word for rabbit), but in the 18th century it was Conig's Castle, probably deriving from a Saxon name.

Continue along the path in the ditch, which has small old oak trees and fine ferns. On the left is a big modern hedge bank with beeches on top, probably dating from the 18th century. *Bear right when the ditch becomes shallower and go on up to a wooden stile by the road. Don't go over the stile, but turn right up the path into the middle of the hillfort.* The grassy and wooded interior shows no original features. *Walk along the path running inside the rampart. This joins a rutted track. Turn right along the track,* which leads towards a shallow hollow which was used as a gravel pit in the 19th century. The gravel taken out here, and the stones lying around here and on Lambert's are all chert, a rough-looking and often pale form of flint.

Walk on around the shallow overgrown gravel pit, bearing left along the path back to the road. Go over the wooden stile, across the road and through a gap in the roadside bank opposite and a little to the right. The modern road cuts straight through the middle of the hillfort, and has destroyed the original entrances.

Go left into the field, and along the hedge bank (right) and at the end of the hedge bank turn left along the top of the steep slope. This is the edge of the hillfort, with virtually no Iron Age defences on this side because the slope makes it impregnable.

The views from here are vast – Charmouth and the sea to the south (left) and Devon along the horizon straight ahead. We know the names of the Iron Age tribes because they were recorded by Roman writers, and Devon (with Cornwall) was inhabited by a tribe called Dummonii. They had more in common with the Iron Age inhabitants of Brittany than with the rest of Britain. Dorset, including Coney's and Lambert's Castles, was held by the Durotriges. Although our two hillforts are close to the borders between the two tribes they do not seem to be particularly significant or large – much larger hillforts are found further into Dorset.

Walk along the edge of the steep slope, and then left alongside the big bank which runs across the field. Go through the modern gap in the bank and down the steep slope. The hillfort bank and ditch are impressive here. *Walk diagonally downhill across the little field beyond, to the far side,* which has another steep bank and ditch. This encloses another area, probably a big entrance added later in the Iron Age to the original hillfort.

The Marshwood Vale from Pilsdon Pen

Walk back up the field and go through the gateway in the hedge on your right onto the road (B). *Turn right, and walk downhill along the road for about ¼ mile (½km).* Good thick hedgerows here. *Take the first road to the right* (C), *signed Great Coombe Farm. Walk along this road to the farm.* The settlement pattern in this valley is medieval: the valleys would certainly have been farmed in Iron Age times, but the landscape and settlements would have been different. Much of the area was probably grazing, as it is today, but in the Iron Age it would have been unfenced, and possibly bordered by more woodland. There would have been farms in the valley, with small arable fields, but none have yet been located in this area – 2,000 years of farming has obscured them.

Keep on the road which passes through several gates by the farm, and then becomes a gravel track. Walk on up the track, past barns at Higher Coombe, then uphill past the entrance to Little Coombe Farm. The hedges here are full of wild flowers in spring and early summer. *The gravel track joins the road at a complex of two junctions (D). Go straight across towards the National Trust signboard visible ahead and slightly uphill. A gravel path waymarked 'Liberty Trail' and 'Wessex Ridgeway' leads steeply uphill, through a wooden gate and then on uphill.* The 'gravel' of this path is the local chert and there are many plants of sandy soils – broom is one of the most prominent. *The path bears slightly left.* Good sea views. *As the gradient eases follow the hedge bank as it turns to the left and keep on this path through open ground and then woody scrub. At the path crossroads, keep straight on towards the hedgerow of big beeches.* This large grassy area was a horse racing course in the 19th century. *At the National Trust car park* (E) *(on the line of the beeches) turn right,* but first look to the left to see the huge hedge bank going on down the hill. *Keep on the wide grassy path running along the edge of the open ground with woods on the left. The path goes slightly uphill, and the banks of Lambert's Castle hillfort come into view. Walk on to the entrance gap and up into the bank.* Lambert's defences are less impressive than Coney's, with just a single bank and ditch of small size. The area enclosed is a little bigger than Coney's Castle, and Lambert's is on a higher hill (839ft, 255m at the centre) rather overlooking Coney's. It is unusual to have two hillforts so close together, particularly as both are small and simple and therefore probably early.

Walk across the middle of the hillfort towards the woods. The little bank and ditch on the left is a modern field boundary. The rather more prominent little hump on the right is probably a Bronze Age round barrow, pre-dating the hillfort. Small rectangular humps show the lines of footings for small buildings, probably used by the fairs held here twice a year from medieval times until the early 20th century.

Keep on through the middle of the fort bearing slightly left at the far edge of the open space – as the path starts to go downhill towards the woods it becomes clearer. In the little fields to the right a telegraph station was built in the early 19th century, part of a line connecting Plymouth to London.

At the fence (F), don't take the path downhill, but turn right along the fence, at the edge of the woods. The hedge bank just inside the fence is on top of the Iron Age rampart, and the ditch is outside the bank. Not particularly impressive. *Keep on along the path inside the fence.* A hedge bank running across the fort joins the defences at a right angle, and beyond the Iron Age bank and ditch are clearer because there is no hedge bank on top. *The path along the fence turns and drops into the Iron Age ditch, with the rampart to the right. Continue along here.*

Picturesque glimpses of the Marshwood Vale through the trees on the left. A few huge old beeches. *Continue along the path in the ditch until the path and ditch turn to the right. Go up the steep little path right to the top of the rampart.* We are now back close to the entrance of the hillfort.

Huge view over Dorset from the top of the rampart and benches to admire it from. To the left the steep nose on the horizon marks the next nearest hillfort – Pilsdon Pen – which at 908ft (277m) is also the highest point in the county. The wooded hill of Lewesdon is to the right of it, and on the far rim of hills is another hillfort Eggardon, not really distinguishable. Abbotsbury Castle, yet another hillfort, is on the end of the ridge on the horizon as it meets the sea, and beyond is the peninsula of Portland. A patchwork of fields fills the Marshwood Vale.

We now leave the hillfort and head back downhill towards the path we came up on.

Walk along the top of the rampart to the entrance, go out through the entrance, left into the ditch and then immediately right along the path running southwards along the hillside. This joins a more prominent path. Coney's Castle with its woods is clear in the foreground half left. Very distinctive acid flora here, with heather, birch, rowan and bracken.

The path goes downhill and meets our outward route. Continue downhill on the gravel track, steeply down to the wooden gate. At the road, go straight over the triangular junction, and take the road to the left of the gravel path we came up. The road goes uphill, and we stay on it until we reach Coney's Castle.

The Iron Age was brought to a sudden end in 43AD, when the Romans invaded Britain. The Roman account of the invasion mentions twenty 'oppida' or towns taken during the invasion – some of these would have been the larger hillforts elsewhere in Dorset. Coney's and Lambert's may have been hastily re-fortified at this time, as many were, but since they have not been excavated we cannot be sure. *The road levels out and the car park is on the left.*

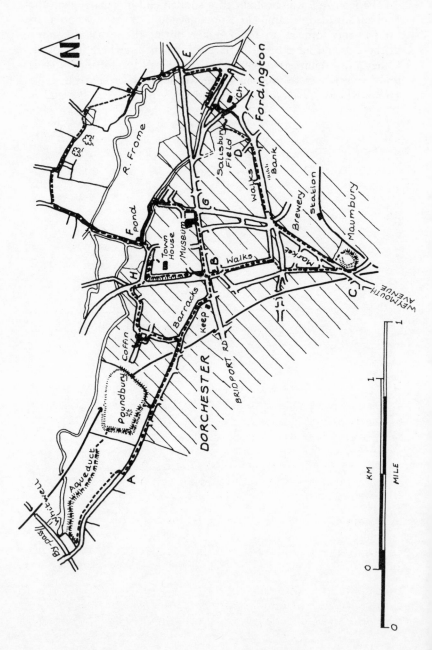

Durnovaria – a Roman Town

A walk around the Roman town of Durnovaria (Dorchester), taking in the Roman defences, the amphitheatre of Maumbury, and the remains of a Roman house, with the Iron Age hillfort of Poundbury, the aqueduct and part of the valley of the Frome. Poundbury and the river valley are surprisingly rural, and the walk goes through the best part of the town. One less interesting suburban part is unavoidable to link Poundbury to the walk. Paths are clear and well-used, but largely not waymarked. The full route is 6 miles (10km); a shortcut offers a shorter route of 5 miles (8½km). This walk could easily be done in stages. The complete route involves 275ft (85m) of climbing, spread out over the whole walk.

Introduction: Durnovaria was the only Roman town in Dorset, and has a surprising number of visible Roman remains. Thomas Hardy claimed that it 'announced old Rome in every street, alley and precinct'. We know the Roman name from a late Roman road-book called the *Antonine Itinerary*. Dorchester was the hub of a number of Roman roads, and was fully urban by about 100AD, with its beginnings soon after the Roman Conquest of 43AD. Many finds from the town can be seen in the Dorset County Museum.

Parking and Public Transport: From the Top O'Town, the roundabout at the western end of the High Street, take the Bridport Road a tiny way west, and turn right by the big stone keep, signposted Industrial estates and TA Centre. Keep along this road. After the buildings cease, go on for 400 yards, past two passing places; and at the crest of the hill is the parking area on the right of the road also marked passing place. Park there (A on the map SY677912). Dorchester is easily accessible by public transport, either by train or bus.

Information: Dorchester town centre has many pubs, cafes, restaurants and so on, plus public lavatories. The Dorset County Museum, High East Street (fee) is open Mon-Sat, 10 a.m. – 5 p.m. all year and also Sundays in July and August (01305 262735).

Directions:
Go through the gate into the open field, turn left and walk parallel with the hedge along the path which has developed a little way out

into the field. All this area around Poundbury has good chalkland flora and butterflies, and wide views across the Frome Valley. *Keep along here, going slightly downhill,* and about halfway along the Roman aqueduct is visible straight ahead on the far hillside, about 1/3 way up, looking like a shelf running along the hillside. The tarmac road straight ahead is on the line of a Roman road, and to the right of it the line of the aqueduct continues as a hedge line.

As the slope steepens the path is in a very marked hollow way, made in medieval times by an earlier course of a road.

Through the hedge at the corner of the field is a good view of the aqueduct contouring along the side of the combe. *Turn right and follow along the hedge.* From 25 yards along, the path follows in the bottom of the aqueduct, with a short steepish slope to the right. The big ditch which carried the water is mostly silted up, but it is still impressive. Where the hedge stops, look downhill to see the big spring of Whitwell, which emerges here and runs almost immediately into the Frome.

Continue walking along the shelf which marks the aqueduct. Water was brought from at least 3 miles upstream to the top of the Roman town. With the River Frome (here below us) at the bottom of the town, this seems extravagant, but the aqueduct supplied clean water at enough pressure to serve even the highest parts of Dorchester. The town did not have such a good water supply again until the 1850s, when Whitwell (the spring we saw earlier) was considered and rejected as the main source. Artesian wells in the chalk were preferred.

Keep on along the aqueduct as it contours along the hillside towards the hillfort. The brick walls on the left are a late 19th century pistol range, used by the barracks. *Keep on along the aqueduct until it meets a wire fence. The top bank on the skyline is the Iron Age hillfort – the aqueduct continues along below the fort, but at the far end of this side of the fort it cuts the defences.*

Turn right, up the slope to a stile, go over and straight ahead, past the first bank, and up onto the second bank. On the river side the hillfort has only a single bank, but on this more vulnerable side there are two, the outer one probably added later in the Iron Age. *Walk along the top of the bank.* About 2/3 of the way along two dips, one with iron showing in the bottom, probably represent Second World War occupation. *At the corner, go down and up to the bank again.* This entrance is modern. The first part of the bank over the entrance was re-used as an Observer Corps look-out post in the Second World War, and odd pieces of ironwork still protrude from the ground.

The prominent mound inside the hillfort is a Bronze Age barrow predating the fort, and beside it on the far side a square parchmark shows in dry summers, indicating the footings of a building which may have been a Roman temple, like the one excavated at Maiden Castle. The hillforts were deserted after the Roman invasion, and the empty enclosures made good sites for temples. A small Iron Age settlement running down the hill towards Dorchester continued to be occupied throughout the Roman period. The long ramparts of Maiden Castle are visible just below the skyline to the right – they dwarf those here.

Go down the bank at the gap, which is another modern entrance – the only Iron Age entrance is in the next rampart along. *Head right for the iron gate, go through the kissing gate and turn left down the road. First downhill, and then back up to the bridge over the railway.* This area was a Prisoner-of-War camp in the First World War, and then an Army Camp in the Second World War. It is now an industrial estate. The exotic looking tower on the skyline to the right is the water tower for the 1850s water supply for the town. The brick arch visible up the railway line is for the tunnel which takes the line under the hillfort, deliberately planned to preserve the archaeology.

Keep on along the road, passing through the barrack area. At the junction look right up Bridport Road, one of the many Roman roads running into Dorchester. *Turn left towards the roundabout and cross over the road. At the roundabout cross over Albert Road.* Look to the left to see the line of Colliton Walk, part of the Roman defences laid out as a tree-lined walk in the 18th century. *Turn right, and 25 yds along* (B) is the railed-in remnant of the stone wall which was built in the 3rd century right round the Roman town, on top of the earlier earthen defences. The wall was robbed for building stone from Saxon times until the 17th century, and this pitiful portion is just the core, with all the fine facing stones gone. It was originally 25ft (8m) high, and would have had stone gates at the entrances to the town, all long gone.

Facing the wall, turn right, and cross the road into West Walks, another part of the tree-lined promenade on the defences. Until the late 19th century Dorchester's built-up area was confined within the Roman defences, but after 1876 it expanded beyond them. The public gardens on the right were laid out in the 1890s on the site of part of the Roman ditch – the distinct dip is still clear. *Keep on down West Walks,* and at the corner look left down Bowling Alley Walk, which continues the line of the defences. *Turn right along the path by the gardens, and at the main road turn left across the*

High East Street, Dorchester

road and straight on up Maumbury Road. Keep on to the junction, cross over, and head right then immediately left and through the gate to the grassy banks (C). Go up the steps to the left, up onto the bank. Maumbury was the amphitheatre for the Roman town, but it was not a new construction – the Romans adapted an old earthwork. Excavations here from 1908 proved that Maumbury was first a Neolithic henge, then a Roman amphitheatre, and finally a Civil War fort. The remodelling of 1642 produced the ramps inside, which were used to trundle guns to the tops of the banks. Turn right and walk on around the top of the bank. Maumbury is unlikely to have seen gladiators (these only starred at larger places), but wild beast shows and circuses would have been staged. The railway runs in a steep curve from Dorchester station (visible from the bank) deliberately so as to avoid Maumbury. Good chalkland flora here. Go down the steps at the entrance, which is the original, and straight ahead to the gate. Out into Weymouth Avenue, on the route of another Roman road, and turn right. Keep on down this road, passing the market (laid out in the 1870s) on the left and the County Police Station of 1860 on the right, with the huge brewery (1880s and 1920s) below it. *At the five-way junction, turn right across Prince of Wales Road, then straight ahead over the pedestrian crossing.* Turn right to go along perhaps the finest of the Walks, South or Chestnut Walks. The Roman (and modern) town is to the left. *Keep on along here. Go across a side road* and look to the right – the grassy bank is a well-preserved part of the Roman defences. *Keep on along the Walk to the corner,* which has three statues by Elisabeth Frink on the site of the gallows.

Cross over Icen Way, straight ahead (D), and take the path leading slightly to the left towards the open field. The tree-lined walk continues to the left, *but we take the winding gravel path, half right, leading along the side of Salisbury Field,* a recreation ground since the 1890s. The iron cage on the right encloses a fundamental bench mark of the Ordnance Survey. *As the path heads left, near the corner of the field, turn right to an alley between modern flats and a Victorian terrace. Go up this alley (brick wall on the left), and soon left to emerge in a road by a fine Georgian house.* This is Fordington, now a suburb of Dorchester, but once a separate medieval village. *Turn right, cross over the road and walk to the church gate.* Fordington Green is on the right. *Go up the path to the church* (fine late medieval tower, most of the rest harsh early 20th century) and go inside to see, reset under the tower, the tombstone of Carinus, a Roman citizen who was buried in the second century in the huge Roman burial ground which runs down the hill towards Dorchester from the area of the church. The inscription records that he was 50, and the stone was set up by his children Rufinus, Carina and Avita and his wife Romana. More than 300 burials have been found in the area since the 18th century, but all were found too early for proper excavation. The coincidence of a Roman burial ground and an early medieval church has led to suggestions that Fordington had a late Roman Christian church, set close to the graves of Christian martyrs, as at St Albans. No proof has yet been found.

Return to Fordington Green from the church, and turn right, retracing your steps. Go down Pound Lane, the first turning to the right, leading downhill. Go left at the junction and immediately right over the road and down the brick steps to the river. This part of Fordington was the Mixen Lane in Thomas Hardy's *Mayor of Casterbridge,* densely occupied by the poor and a hotbed of disease. Now rebuilt, it is unrecognisable. *Go over the bridge, turn right and walk along Mill Lane.* Huge mill of 1891 at the end, the river and bridge picturesque in front. This was the main way into Dorchester until the 18th century. *Turn left, keep along the road to junction at the main road.* The austere classical stone bridge (E) on the right was built in 1748 – the straight road running left to the old town of Dorchester is of the same date, not Roman as it appears to be. A Roman road approaching Dorchester from the east is clearly visible in Thorncombe Woods, but the line it took across the river valley is not known.

[To shorten the walk, leaving out the walk up the valley, turn left up the road and continue halfway up the High Street to the Dorset County Museum, just above St Peter's church].

Cross the main road, go over the bridge and immediately left through the metal kissing gate onto the riverside path. Keep on along this path, over the bridge with metal sluices, through trees, over a little bridge and past a thatched cottage. Go over the stile beyond the cottage, and then diagonally across the open field heading for the right hand side of the farm buildings.

The landscape of the Frome valley we walk through is medieval, and bears no relationship to the Roman landscape. Sections dug in the river valley near the Dorchester bypass show that in the Iron Age the river valley was pasture, but in Roman times peat was forming. The present courses of the river are medieval, designed to supply all the mills with water.

At the farm buildings join a track, go left through a gate and on along the track. Straight over at the next junction, along a path at the edge of the field. Lots of trees in the fields all through here, and many small woods. *The path becomes a track by a cottage: straight on, right at the junction for 20 yards and then left through a wooden kissing gate in the hedge and straight ahead along the fence.* Good view of Dorchester to the left, with the town steadily sloping down its hill. *Go through the kissing gate and turn left down the gravel track.* The watersplash across the track is part of the supply system for the watermeadows. *Keep on down the track, over another watersplash to a metal bridge over the river.* Complicated meeting of river channels here. *Keep on straight ahead to a round pond and another part of the river (F) and turn left along the riverside path. At the first bridge* (by a cottage on the site of one of the medieval mills) *cross over the river and go straight ahead up the hill into the town.* Excavations at the top of the hill showed that there was at least one ditch defending the river side of the Roman town. *Bear to the right, heading for the church (G).* The centre of medieval and modern Dorchester may be close to the centre of the Roman town, although the High Streets are on a slightly different alignment from the Roman roads. The forum may have been here, but since excavations in the centre have been limited to tiny trenches we cannot be sure.

The memorial to Thomas Hardy

Turn right at the High Street and walk up to the Dorset County Museum, just above the church. Go into the museum (fee) to see three big mosaics from Roman Dorchester on the floor of the Victorian gallery and the exhibition gallery, and upstairs the archaeological displays. Look particularly at the material on Maumbury, Colliton Park Roman town house and the aqueduct.

Leaving the museum, turn right up High West Street, and at the top (the roundabout) turn right down Colliton Walk (statue of Thomas Hardy on the left). The road below is in the silted-up ditch of the Roman defences, and the bank is very impressive here. *Walk to the corner* (H), *and turn right keeping along the top of the bank.*

Halfway along this part, turn right through a gate at the signpost 'Roman town house'. The flint footings of a complex Roman house are preserved and exposed here. Large-scale excavations in the 1930s, before County Hall was built, revealed this house and other less substantial buildings. The house was originally tucked up into the corner of the defences, but earthmoving since the 1930s for the new buildings has left it in a deep hollow. The remains date from the 3rd and 4th centuries, with a pleasing mosaic preserved under the little roof. The reconstructed column is part of a veranda – most of the nine broken columns were found in the well close by.

Go out the way you came in, turn left, retracing your steps to the corner of the defences (H), and then go down the ramp to the road. Cross over, go right and then left at the first junction (signposted 'The Grove and Marabout Industrial Estates'). *Keep on along this road, ignoring the left turn.* This was also part of the Army Camp. *The road turns left, and immediately afterwards to the right, up another road to the factory of Wyvern Fireplaces* which has displayed outside a Hamstone coffin with lid, one of over 1,400 Roman burials excavated here from the 1960s. Like all the area around Dorchester (apart from the riverside) this was farmland in the early Roman period, but in the fourth century a small cemetery here was hugely extended and the farms went out of use, the land being taken over for burial. Most of the graves were laid out with the head to the west and few or no gravegoods, suggesting that the cemetery was Christian. The stone coffin here is one of ten found: most of them had plaster packing inside to try to preserve the body.

Turn round and walk a little downhill and take the first right and then first left, returning to the major road through the industrial estate, lined on the far side with walnut trees. *Turn right (uphill) and at the top of the hill turn right and walk along the road, past Poundbury, to the car park.*

A Saxon Boundary at Tarrant Hinton

Most of the parish boundary of Tarrant Hinton still follows the line described in a 10th century charter. This walk follows the most accessible part of the boundary, and goes through a well wooded area. We walk part of the boundary of Eastbury Park, through woods and tree lined droves, across Chettle Park and back across more open farmland to the village, returning up the shallow river valley. Only a few of the paths are way-marked, but they are all easy to find. The walk is undulating, with no severe slopes. The route is 4½ miles (7½km), with 250 ft (75m) of climbing.

Introduction: The pattern of villages in Dorset was established after the Saxons invaded the county in the 7th century AD Most village names date from 7th-10th centuries, and even more surprisingly, some charters survive giving boundaries which still match present boundaries. Only a small proportion of the charters issued survive, and this is usually because they were incorporated into later ones. The Tarrant Hinton charter used here was granted in 935AD, when King Athelstan gave Shaftesbury Abbey lands at Tarrant Hinton. It survives as a 13th century copy, which was discarded when Shaftesbury Abbey was abolished (with all the other monasteries) in the 1530s, but was acquired by one of the two Earls of Oxford (both great collectors) in the late 17th or early 18th century. Nearly fifteen thousand charters, deeds and other manuscripts belonging to them (including this one) were one of the first acquisitions of the British Museum when it was founded in 1753.

Parking and public transport: Drive to Tarrant Hinton village, just north of the A354 Blandford-Salisbury road. Drive north through the village and on for ½ mile to where a track joins from the left, just before an S bend (A on the map ST931109). Park carefully out of the way of the track on the wide verge where track and road join. The walk is possible by bus as Salisbury-Blandford and Salisbury-Weymouth buses pass along the main road. The nearest pub is in Tarrant Gunville village, just to the north. No other refreshments, lavatories etc. on the route. Chettle House (fee) is open daily except Tues and Sat, mid April – early October (01258 – 830209).

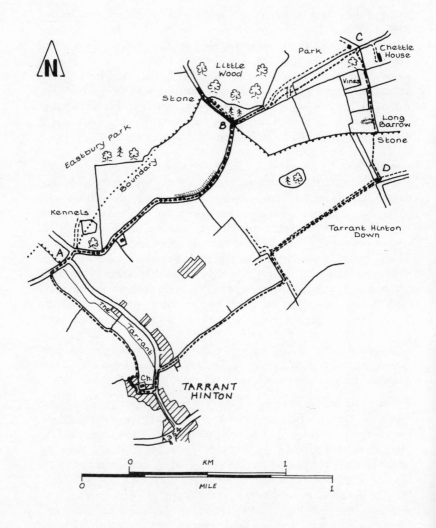

Directions:

Walk along the road to the S bend, towards the elegant stone gatepiers in the well-treed hedge. The road is on the Saxon boundary, which starts at Pimperne Spring, as Tarrant Hinton included a big area to the south of Pimperne, then heads north and turns to the east to reach this point. It continues on the same alignment as the road into Eastbury Park, but the line there has been obscured by the kennels built just inside the park in the early 19th century by John James Farquarson, a famous huntsman. The gatepiers are part of Eastbury House, a huge mansion built from 1717 and designed by Vanburgh. It measured 570ft across the main front, and was so large that no tenant could be found in the 1770s, and it was demolished. A small part, including the original kitchen, still survives, along with the gates.

Turn right up the No Through Road, and keep on along this road, which runs along the boundary of Eastbury Park. The ornamental trees, mostly planted in the 18th century, are now huge and old. The 18th century Dorset historian Hutchins recorded that some mature trees were planted, brought from 'some miles off after fiftey years' growth' and weighing ten tons.

When you reach a house on the right, look through the gap in the hedge on the left to see over the park. It has been ploughed since 1958, and the Saxon boundary, which ran up the middle parallel to our road, is only visible when the fields are bare.

Keep on up the road, which becomes a gravel track, and passes through trees of many different varieties, doubtless planted by the owners of the big house. *Keep on along the grassy track, which declines to a path after it turns to the left a little.* Parts of the brick wall of the park survive on the left, and beyond is a bank, part of a big Iron Age settlement which extends into the field on the right, all the way around and beyond the clump of trees. Until the field was ploughed earthworks of the settlement survived over a large area of downland.

The path emerges from the trees. The hedge ahead on the left is the Saxon boundary. *Go through the gate at the end of the path, and we join the boundary* (B). *Turn left up the track, walking parallel with the part of the boundary* described in 935 as 'an lang there Fures on that Dich' meaning 'along the Furrow to the Dyke'. The low double bank in the hedge is the Dyke and must have been part of the Iron Age settlement. Saxon boundaries often use earlier earthworks as landmarks, especially in areas of open grazing like this downland. The plantation on the right is modern, *but after ignoring a track from the left, we soon reach Little Wood,* which amazingly is still known by the name it had in 935 – continuity of name and vegetation for 1,000 years is impressive. A little further on, on the left by the iron railings, is a 1ft high boundary stone which marks the corner of the present parish and the Saxon one. The stone is probably 19th century. *Walk a little way further up the track* until you can see through the scrub and railings on the left – the boundary is the slight bank with one tree on it, running at right angles. It passes right through the park, to emerge at the entrance where we started the walk. The Saxon description of the part across the park is 'along the Highway as far as the Little Wood' (Littlen Wood in the original). The road probably existed until Eastbury Park was created – the route we came by was probably then substituted.

Turn round and retrace your steps back along the boundary (on the right this time) to the gate and junction where we joined it (B).

The boundary continues on the same line along the hedge straight ahead, heading for 'Tata's Barrow', which still survives. Barrows were prominent markers, often used by boundaries.

We turn left, down the dirt track (waymarked Jubilee Trail) with Little Wood on the left. Keep on along this track, through a wicket gate by a field gate and into parkland ornamented by large old trees. This is the park of Chettle House. *Keep on straight ahead on the grassy track.* The Saxon boundary is running along the hedge on the skyline to the right. *Go straight over at the junction of tracks and*

Chettle House

keep on along the grassy path through the park. Just before the wooden gate at the junction of several paths (C), turn right (blue arrow painted on the tree) down an open grassy path which winds through big trees. [If you want to visit Chettle House, don't turn right, but go through the gate and then right].

A little way on, we pass very close to Chettle House (left), a sophisticated little mansion of 1710. *Go through the wooden gate straight ahead and on uphill on a wide grassy track along the side of the field* (vines on the right) *with the hedge on our left.* Lovely view of the trees we have been walking through to the right.

On through two gates, and then on our right is a huge Neolithic long barrow, at right angles to the path. The Saxon boundary is a little further on, and was following a highway and so could afford to ignore this prominent landmark.

Keep on to the next hedgerow which is the Saxon boundary, heading along a road (now moved south to the present main road) towards the river at Chettle. *Go through the hedge* and on the left hand side of the path as it goes through, is another small boundary stone – this one inscribed A H C.

Turn half right to go diagonally across the field ahead, making for a white post and stile visible in the hedge. Don't go over the stile, but after reaching it continue down the hedge line to reach a gravel road at the corner of the field (D). Turn right and keep on along this road. This is Tarrant Hinton Down, ploughed only this century. The hedge on the skyline to the right is the Saxon boundary. The boundary returns to Pimperne after defining the circuit of Tarrant Hinton parish, to the Pimperne stream. The 'Burnestowe' at Pimperne it is described as passing was translated as 'the holy place of the Bourne' in the 1930s, but is now thought to be the more prosaic 'watering place for cattle'. The area is currently used for pigs. *At the top of the hill where roads join, turn left along the hedge running along the top of the hill, and then first right. Keep on straight ahead and down the hill.* The lower part has been arable cultivation for a long time, possibly since Saxon times. When the Tithe map was made in 1839 the parish was half arable and half downland, with a small area of woods.

Keep on down the hill towards the village, going through a metal gate and on down a track to the road. Turn left along this road. The thatched brick, flint or cob cottages date from the 16th to the 19th centuries, but are on sites which were used by the Saxon village. *After the post-box, turn right up the No Through Road.* Worth visiting the church, which is late medieval, to see the very early classical Easter Sepulchre with its fine stone carving (of about 1536, to the left of the altar) and the very stylish iron and brass lectern of 1909. The Saxon church was almost certainly on this site, but nothing remains of it.

Turn right up the road after visiting the church, and keep on up here past a No Access notice (there is a right of way on foot) *and through by the cottages. At the Rectory gate turn to the left (waymarked), along a path between two hedges. Where this emerges into the field, turn right and walk downhill along the hedge to the corner. Turn left and continue straight along, with the hedge on your right, working up the valley.* The River Tarrant is in the bottom of the shallow valley to the right: although the name is first recorded in Saxon times, its origin is earlier. Like many river names it is Celtic, a variation of Trent whose literal meaning is probably trespasser, a river which floods. The Tarrant is empty much of the year, but still causes floods in the winters. It has given its name to eight villages hereabouts.

The big house visible straight ahead is Gunville House, built in the 1790s from materials taken from Eastbury, then being demolished. *We emerge through a metal gate, turn right, and the car is parked a little way on the left.*

The Vikings at Wareham

A walk around the impressive Saxon defences of Wareham, through the water-meadows, and across farmland to Poole Harbour. The full walk is 6 miles (9½km) but a shortened version of 5 miles (7½km) is offered, and it can even be cut down to 3 miles (5km). The only climbing is the town defences – this is a level walk. The paths are clear and easy apart from the two mile riverside path, which is only for the adventurous. The alternative route to the riverside part is easy and well-marked. Very varied countryside, full of birds, but likely to be severely altered by gravel extraction in the future.

Introduction: Wareham was founded in Saxon times and has more remains of that period than any other place in Dorset, with the town walls (really a bank), one Saxon church and parts of another. We also have many references to Wareham in the few documents which survive from this period, showing that the town played an important role in Southern England's battle to repulse the Vikings. Wareham was part of the kingdom of Wessex – England did not yet exist and was sub-divided into several areas at this time.

Parking and Public Transport: Drive to Wareham and park in the long-stay car park on the west of the town by the town walls (A on the map). The road to the car park is opposite the Purbeck District Council Offices on the main road in from Dorchester and is signed 'Wareham Hospital, Ambulance Station, Health Centre'. One has to pay to park here: out of season you may be able to park for free on one of the side streets of Wareham. Wareham can be reached easily by public transport: trains on the Bournemouth-Weymouth line (walk towards the centre of Wareham, and join the walk at St Martin's church) or buses from Dorchester, Poole or Wimborne to the centre of the town (walk along West Street to West Walls to start the walk).

Information: Lavatories, pubs, cafes, restaurants in the centre of Wareham. Well worth visiting Wareham Museum, by the Town Hall (free, open Easter-mid October, Mon – Sat 10-1 and 2-5 (01929 553448).

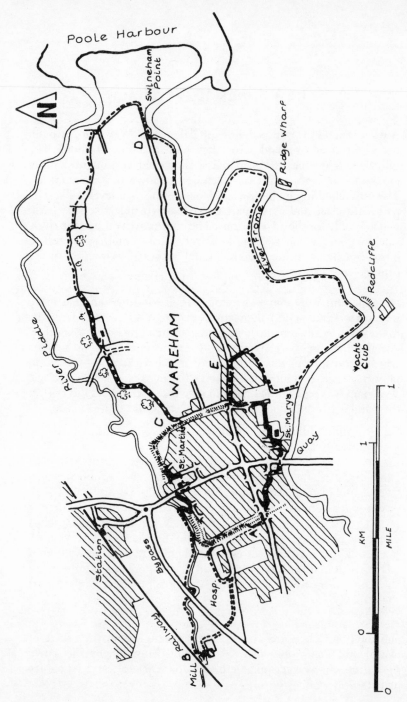

Poole Harbour

Swineham Point

Ridge Wharf

River Frome

Redcliffe

Yacht Club

D

E

WAREHAM

River Piddle

C

St. Martins

St. Marys

Quay

Station

Bypass

Hosp.

Mill B

Rail - Wareham

KM

MILE

1

1

0

0

Directions:

From the car park, walk up onto the green bank of West Walls, part of the bank which encloses the town on three sides. The bank is Saxon, and certainly existed by 910AD, when it was listed in the Burghal Hidage, a tax list from which a calculation gives the length of the defences. The Wareham defences come out at 2,200 yards, their current size. The exact date they were built is not certain, but it was probably in the 890s, as part of King Alfred's chain of defences to protect Wessex against Viking attacks. Vikings from Scandinavia had been raiding the Dorset coast since 789AD, and by the middle of the 9th century were a serious threat to the Kingdom of Wessex. In 876 an army of 2,000 Vikings over-wintered at Wareham, and it may be that the defences already existed at that time. The Vikings were ejected by Alfred (partly by treachery) and by luck their fleet of ships was destroyed by a storm off Swanage. The Vikings, in their short stay, had devastated a large area around in their search for loot, but the defeat at Wareham marked the turning point: Alfred succeeded in preventing Viking settlement, and although attacks continued until 896, even these finally ceased.

Walk along the top of the bank, northwards, towards the trees. The bank has been excavated by archaeologists in this area. The ditch is visible outside the bank (the car park and road are within it). The bank was heightened along this side in 1940 as a defence against tanks.

Wareham took a long time to fill the area inside the defences – most of the houses we shall see from the banks are 20th century, like those on the right. The big building visible on the left is the Workhouse, built in 1837. In 1850 parts of the bank were thrown down into the ditch to improve the road to the Workhouse.

At the corner of the bank there is a seat with good views over the River Piddle (or Trent, both names are used). Wareham is set neatly between two rivers, at the point where they virtually cease to be tidal, and at the lowest bridging point. The watermeadows beyond the town are now cut by the bypass.

Don't continue along the bank, but go back a little and turn downhill (right) into the ditch, then right and immediately left a little uphill and through two narrow gateways out into the open meadows. Keep straight ahead, along beside a row of pine trees. We are on the gravel ridge here, clearly showing its height above the meadows. *The path goes along the ridge, and then downhill keeping parallel with a stream. Join the gravel road and continue to the right towards the bypass.* The watermeadows are rich in flowering plants, proper unimproved grassland, and mostly divided into plots by branches of the river.

Go under the bypass, and keep on straight along the gravel road to the mill. The river is wide and picturesque here. *Go through the gate into the yard, and turn right to pass in front of the mill* (B). Several millstones are displayed in front – some of them composites made from many small pieces of stone. Paper was made here from the 17th century until about 1830 – mills provided power for many processes as well as grinding corn. The late 18th century building was converted to flats recently. There could have been a mill here in medieval or even Saxon times. The building is completely surrounded by water – partly the mill stream, partly the river. The embankment ahead is the railway line. *Go through the metal gate to the right and then along the path parallel to the river.*

Wareham's name is first recorded in 786AD as Werham, the 'homestead by the weir'. This does not mean a mill, but a weir used to trap fish. Later documents make it clear that both Wareham rivers had these weirs, but the largest and earliest one was probably on the Frome, the other side of the town. Salmon were the main fish caught, and they are still found in the river today.

Follow the path by the river under the bypass, and along below the north walls of the town (the seat we looked out from earlier is visible on top). *Go over the sluices for another mill, and soon right, over a pretty little brick bridge.* The buildings ahead are North Mill, first mentioned in documents in 1150, when it belonged to the prior of Wareham. The present buildings are mostly 18th century. *Go up the steep tarmac drive* – this is the defensive bank – *and turn left at the road, going downhill to the main road.* 18th and 19th century houses here, on one of the main roads of Wareham. *Turn right along the main road, and soon cross over the road to get to St Martin's church.* St Martin's church is on top of the defences and next to the northern entrance to the town. Externally the little 16th century tower dominates. (The top rebuilt 1712 and dated). Inside the nave and chancel (and even the chancel arch) are all very late Saxon, dating from just before the 11th century Norman conquest. This simple building survived the Victorian restoration mania because it was not used as a church at that time. The elegant tomb with figure is a memorial to Lawrence of Arabia (see Walk no.15).

Turn left when leaving the church, along the tree-lined path to a road. Turn left, and then right at the end of the road, up onto the bank. Walk along the bank to the corner. The open area inside the town has a rectangular enclosure on the far side, surrounded by a low bank. This was called the bowling green in the 17th and 18th centuries, and was used for fairs.

St Martin's Church, Wareham

Turn right and continue along the top of the bank into some trees (C). [If you wish to take the very short route, keep on along the bank, until East Street is reached, and rejoin the walk at East Walls]. *Turn left steeply down the bank to the road, turn left and continue along the road.* This area is called Bestwall, a name recorded at Doomsday (1086) and meaning 'by east walls'. The road runs through a narrow belt of woodland, with views of the River Piddle and its marshy valley to the left. *Cross the new road, built for gravel extraction, and continue along the road ahead. Soon after, as the road turns right, continue straight on along a dirt track. When this ends, bear left over a wooden stile by a gate, turn right and out into the meadows.* An unusual landscape, wide open, remote and flat, running to Poole Harbour, with herds of cows wandering about. *Walk along the path parallel to the woodlands. This path turns right, crosses a bridge and continues parallel with the woods. Keep straight ahead and at the corner of the field, go over the stile, and follow the path to the right which runs along the edge of the reeds.* Small paths lead out through the reeds to the River Piddle. *Ignore these, and continue to the end of the grassy path. Take the stile on the left leading into the reeds, and follow the path between the hedge and the reeds.* The saltmarsh and reeds to the left is Swineham Point, which borders Poole Harbour. The hedge here, and all around the field to the right is on a bank to keep the sea off the grazing land.

Stop on the corner, where the path turns right. This is an unusual view of Poole Harbour. To the right the hills are those of Arne, with little cliffs to the shore. The other cliffs straight ahead are Rockley Sands, near Poole.

The river visible ahead is the Frome – Viking ships would have used this route to reach Wareham, rowing their shallow-draught open vessels up the river. Now its course can be traced by masts of pleasure vessels sticking up above the reeds.

The path turns right, on the bank still, and meets the river. Go past a stile, and continue on the bank (D). [The track to the right leads back to Wareham and is the recommended route for those who don't want to push their way through reeds all along the river bank. Rejoin the main route at E].

The river path is for the adventurous – there are reeds all the way, like a jungle, some taller than you are, and attentive brambles. Because of the bends in the river, the route is twice as long as the shortcut offered above. *Continue along the river path, with glimpses of the river.* Lots of birds. Ridge Wharf, on the opposite side is now a yacht centre, but was built in about 1860 as the terminus to a tramway which carried clay from pits inland to the river. The clay was tipped into barges and towed to Poole.

Keep on along the riverside path. The isolated hump of sandstone forming Redcliffe has a cliff to the riverside, and a Yacht Club on the far side, in a wooden building. *Eventually the path turns right, away from the river, leading through reeds and scrub to the back of housing, turns right along the back of the houses (well-marked and with stiles). Turn left at the end of the path and through two gates to reach the road* (E). (Those who flinched at the riverside path rejoin here). *Turn left along the road, and walk through suburban development until East Walls, the green bank marking the edge of the Saxon town, is reached.*

Turn left and climb up East Walls, walk along and then down the far end, keeping straight on along the road ahead. Turn right at the end, along the tarmac road through the churchyard. Turn left to go into the church. On top of the tower of about 1500 the windvane is a gilded salmon. Until 1841 this church had a huge Saxon nave, just the same size as the current one. This was demolished and rebuilt in a style more acceptable to the Victorians. The date of the parts they demolished is difficult to determine: from drawings we can be sure it was Saxon, but documentary evidence is difficult to match with it. In 802 a king of the West Saxons was buried here, suggesting that

The Quay and St Mary's Church, Wareham

there was already a church, but it seems unlikely that a church survived the Vikings over-wintering here in 876. Architectural historians cannot agree the exact date of the church, but it seems likely to have been built, or more likely rebuilt, in the late 9th or early 10th century. During the demolition five stones with inscriptions on were discovered: these are Celtic in style and probably date from the 5th-7th centuries, coming from a graveyard which existed before the Saxon church was built. Like the church, historians have argued about the date for the stones, some suggesting that they are as late as the 9th or 10th century. These odd stones are displayed in the left hand corner of the church, towards the chancel. The memorial stone to John Hutchins, who was rector here and who published his huge history of Dorset in 1774, is in the chapel to the right of the chancel.

Coming out of the church, go straight across the little green and left into the Quay. The area to the south of the church was the Priory, probably founded in the 8th or 9th century: the earliest parts of the surviving buildings are 16th and 17th century.

The Quay is now used by pleasure boats, but until the early 20th century was commercial, with a big warehouse on the left (now the

Old Granary). The river seems small to have supported so much traffic, but before the railways were built, Wareham had a large trade along the river. (Pubs, cafes and lavatories here). *Walk to the main road, cross over, and down the road opposite.* This is Abbot's Quay, which belonged to Sherborne Abbey. *Turn right as the road turns, along Tanners Lane.* Opposite the junction at the end of the road is Wareham Rectory, where John Hutchins, author of the first big history of Dorset lived, marked by a blue plaque.

Turn left into Pound Lane, past the Old Brewery (now flats) and the brick wall enclosing Castle Close, the site of the medieval castle, *and on to the main road. The car park is visible opposite.* Worth walking to the centre of the town and visiting Wareham Museum (by the Town Hall) for more information on the town.

Medieval Monks at Abbotsbury

A fairly short walk, with many interesting buildings and good views. One short steepish part up, and another down, but with good, well-marked paths all the way. The longest version is 4 miles (6km), but short-cuts give alternative 1½ miles (2½km) or 3 mile (4½km) routes. The main route goes up 360ft (110m), but not all at once.

The walk goes through Abbotsbury village, up to the isolated chapel of St Catherine, along the coast path to Chesil Bank and back around St Catherine's Hill to the Swannery.

Introduction: Abbotsbury village is famous and popular, full of stone and thatch cottages. The Church, Abbey Barn, St Catherine's Chapel and Swannery are relics from the medieval abbey, and the area is distinctive geographically as well – the little hills and strange lagoon of the Fleet are well worth seeing.

Parking and Public Transport: Park in the large car park outside the Swannery (A on map SY576846), to the south of Abbotsbury village (the Swannery is well sign-posted). Public Transport: buses from Weymouth to the Swannery in July and August, and to Abbotsbury village from Weymouth, Dorchester and Bridport on some days of the week all year.

Information: Lavatories just outside the Swannery and in the middle of the village. Teas at the Swannery, and several cafes and pubs in Abbotsbury village. The Swannery is open to the public (fee) daily March-October, the Tithe Barn (fee) daily same period and Sundays in winter; the Tropical Gardens (fee) daily all year, shorter opening hours in winter.

Directions:
Walk to the entrance of the Swannery. This is the only private herd of swans in the country, and although not mentioned in documents until 1393, probably existed before the Norman Conquest. Originally kept for food (with quills for pens and down for pillows as secondary products), the swans are still looked after by a swanherd. The swannery was one of many monastic rights taken over by the Strangways family who bought the whole estate when the

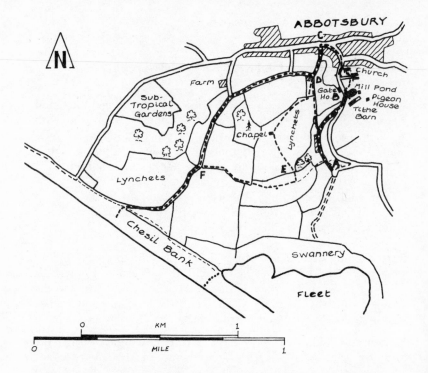

monasteries were abolished in the 16th century. The estate is still owned by the same family.

Turn right at the entrance to the Swannery, up a narrow road signed 'Coast Path – West Bexington and Tithe Barn'. Keep on this little road, which turns into a gravel track and then back to tarmac. A few cottages and the mill house are scattered along this little wooded valley. *Ignore left turn signed St Catherine's Chapel, and continue on uphill along the road to a road junction. Turn left.* The gable end wall of the huge monastic tithe barn has tiny slit windows. *Walk on up the road to the front of the Tithe Barn* (B), which is the largest in the county, built about 1400 by the abbey. Only half is still roofed (and now a museum), but that half is enormous. The barn was not just for tithes, but to store the grain and other crops produced by the abbey on their own lands. Monasteries were huge land-owners in medieval times. Besides 2,000 acres at Abbotsbury, this one owned lands in twelve other parishes, besides houses in Dorchester, Wareham and Bridport. The monks kept up the continuous cycle of services in the church, while lay brothers did most of the manual work. Abbotsbury was founded just before the Norman Conquest. A local historian writing in 1625 recorded the tradition that the abbey was built 'in the verie infancie of Christianitie', having been given to the monks by St Peter, who also provided a charter 'written with his owne Hand'. Even in the 17th century this seemed unlikely. It was really founded by Orc and his wife Tola, followers of King Canute in the 11th century. Abbotsbury was Benedictine, and surviving buildings testify to its riches.

A little way up the road turn right along the path by the pond, then left up the gravel path with steps which leads uphill towards the church. The stone house to the left with big arches in the front wall was the inner gatehouse of the abbey. From the top of the hill is a picture-postcard view back over the pond and barn. In the field behind the barn, to the left, is an isolated building looking like a cottage. It is really a pigeon house, probably built by the abbey, but much altered in the 18th century. These were used to breed pigeons for food.

St Catherine's Chapel is prominent on the hill to the left. Beside the path is a big gable end wall called the Pynion End, dating from

The Tithe Barn, Abbotsbury

about 1400 and part of the abbey buildings. Abbey House (café) to the right and the other houses close by were converted from parts of the abbey. One of the buildings here was the abbey water mill. *Walk on into the churchyard.* On the left of the path (with an explanatory notice) a small part of the footings of the wall of the abbey church are exposed. The church ran south and east from here, and was more than twice the size of the village church. The useful buildings like the barn survived the abolition of the monasteries, but the church was soon demolished.

Walk round the church tower to the porch. Just outside are two medieval coffins, shaped to fit the head, and inside the porch a beautiful memorial to an abbot of about 1200 – a shallowly carved effigy. Just inside the church is a fine drawing reconstructing the abbey buildings. Much of this parish church was here at the time of the abbey – the tower and porch of 1400, and the early 16th-century arches running through the middle of the main body of the church (the arcades). The first two capitals on the south side have initials IP which are probably for John Portesham, Abbot of Abbotsbury 1505-34 (good 17th-century parts including the plaster ceiling in the chancel, wooden pulpit and so on).

Turn left out of the church, down the short path to the road. Turn left along the road. 55 yards (50m) along the start of an arch across the road can be seen in the roadside walls. This was part of the outer gatehouse of the abbey. The wall inside the garden to the right has many carved stones taken from the ruins of the abbey buildings. Several cottages in Abbotsbury have stones like these, set to show the medieval carvings, but this is the best example.

Turn round, walk back past the church gate. The Manor House on the left dates from after the dissolution of the abbey – it is later 16th and 17th century with a pretty porch. The blank wall just beyond it incorporates a blocked up 14th-century window, part of the abbey probably re-set here.

At the road junction continue straight on. Abbotsbury's local stone and thatch cottages are famously picturesque, but mostly date from the 17th and 18th centuries, after the abbey had gone. There was a village here in medieval times, and even a weekly market from 1271, another right owned by the abbey. This street is still called Market Street. *Keep on straight to the middle of the village,* which has many Victorian buildings – the lattice-windowed cottages and the school are the most prominent. The Ilchester Arms is a handsome late 18th century coaching inn, so called because the Strangways heiress married the Earl of Ilchester in the mid 18th century, and the Ilchester and Strangways lands were combined to make one big estate.

Bear left along the main road until Chapel Lane, with a stone indicating that this is the path to St Catherine's Chapel. (C) *Turn left up Chapel Lane, a wide gravel track. Left through the metal kissing gate by farm buildings* (D) *and on up the gravel track signposted St Catherine's Chapel.* The large gardens of the Manor House can be seen in front of the church.

At the bend in the track, go through the kissing gate and follow the sign pointing right up the hill to the chapel across open grassland. The side of the hill ahead is terraced by lynchets, ledges created in the medieval period to make arable cultivation possible on steep slopes. These are some of the finest examples in the county.

St Catherine's Chapel was built about 1400 by the abbey, and survived the abolition of the monasteries because it was useful as a sea-mark. Heavily built, with stone vaulting inside. Traditionally girls looking for a husband could pray to St Catherine one day a year here to supply one: very un-monastic.

Good views across the village to the ridge behind from the chapel. Walk out in front of the chapel to the edge of the hill for the best sea views – right along the Fleet and Chesil Bank. A look-out was posted here in season to watch for shoals of mackerel.

Walk back to the chapel and follow direction of finger-post (indicating 'Swannery' with MacMillan Way marker – see Chesil Beach) diagonally across and down the lynchets to the corner of the wood visible on the left (E). Good view of the Swannery from here, and a closer view of the strange, part salt – part freshwater lagoon of the Fleet stretching along behind Chesil Bank.

[Short cut from here – go over the stile, turn half left downhill towards the car park visible through trees, through metal gate, then over stile to the road, turn right and there is the car park].

Go over the stile and down the rather steep hill to the stone Coast Path marker. Turn right along the coast path, which contours along the hill and is occasionally marked by wooden posts. A concrete pillbox from the Second World War survives by the path, and in the distance, where the Fleet ends, a double row of concrete blocks can be seen running up and over Chesil Bank – a tank stop line also from the Second World War. *Go through the gate at the end of a stone wall, and on along the fence line. At another concrete pillbox beside the path, take the path half left downhill towards the stile visible in the valley. Go over the stile* (F MacMillan Way marker) [If you wish to shorten the walk turn right here up the fenced track and skip three paragraphs to continue directions].

Turn left down the fenced track (signposted 'West Bexington and

T Gardens'), and keep along this path to Chesil Bank. Tamarisk hedges are part of the distinctive seaside greenery. *Go through the wooden gate to the back of the beach,* which has a rich flora including the yellow horned poppy and other seaside specialities.

A patch of reed beds to the left is part of a larger area running along the shores of the Fleet. The reeds have been cut since medieval times for thatching in the village. Some are still cut for that purpose, and other areas maintained as a Nature Reserve for birds. A path through the reed bed leads towards the line of concrete blocks marking the start of the Fleet. Walk down there if you want to see the rare sea pea which grows in the bare shingle (flowering in June/July).

Walk to the top of the shingle bank to see the sea. Hard walking on these stones. Orc, who founded the Abbey in the 11th century was granted all the shore line, with rights of wreck – an unusual privilege preserved by the Strangways. In 1315 the monks successfully claimed a large whale washed up here – normally these rarities belonged to the King. [If you continue along the beach to the right, there may be refreshments in the beach car park. A board walk gives an easy route to the top of Chesil Bank, and is the end of the Mac-Millan Way, a 235 mile footpath which starts at Oakham in the Midlands. The path is routed through limestone areas. To visit the sub-Tropical gardens turn right up the road at the car park. After visiting the gardens continue along the road to Abbotsbury village and follow signs to return to Swannery car park].

Retrace your steps to return up the track we came down. The widely spaced lynchets on the hill to the right below St Catherine's Chapel are clear from this direction. *Ignore the right turn for the chapel* (F), *and keep on the track.* [Shortened route rejoins here]. *Keep along the track, taking next turning to the right through the gate. The track goes uphill a little through trees* and St Catherine's Chapel is visible on the right. *Ignore left turn. Continue straight on towards the church tower along the track, which wriggles slightly right and left. Keep straight on, ignoring turn to right for chapel. We rejoin the outward route at the metal kissing gate* (D) *by farm buildings. Go through the gate, ignore track uphill to the chapel, and take the grassy path leading slightly downhill straight ahead alongside a stone wall. The path goes over a little stream,* which is higher up the river valley than its natural course because a leat has been constructed to bring the water in at a suitable level for the mill just below. *Continue over a stile, on through trees and over a stile in a stone wall to reach the little road. Turn right down the road back to the car park.*

A Medieval Deer Park in the Simene Valley

A walk through the complicated small-scale landscape west of Bridport, over a couple of small hills and across the remote Simene valley, with thick hedges, good wild flowers, birds and butterflies, and intricate views all the way. The route includes several deeply cut, atmospheric hollow ways. The paths can be muddy, but are clear despite being sparsely signposted. Not too strenuous – one easy uphill part, and other shorter ups and downs. The full walk is 4¼ miles (7km) with 500ft (155m) of climbing. The shorter route is 2½ miles (4km).

Introduction: Medieval Dorset had almost fifty deer parks, but few of them are accessible. Symondsbury is a medium size one, whose bounds can be walked. These parks enclosed areas ranging from 70 acres to many hundreds, and had big banks to ensure that the deer stayed inside. The deer were kept for hunting, which was tremendously important in medieval times, partly to supply meat, but equally as a very high status occupation which could only be enjoyed by large land-owners. Venison was a luxury, and poaching was always a problem.

Parking and Public Transport: Drive to Symondsbury, west of Bridport. Park near the church – plenty of space by the triangle with the tree, or up the road beside the church (A on the map SY444945). Difficult by bus, but they do pass along the main road to the south of the village.

Information: No lavatories or cafes on the route, but there is a pub in Symondsbury. Lavatories, cafes and so on in Bridport 1 mile (2km) east.

Directions:
Take the road leading slightly uphill from the tiny triangular green.
In the 13th and 14th centuries when the deer park was in use, Symondsbury was (and still is) a huge parish, running from almost Broadoak in the north right down to the sea. Agriculture was concentrated in the open fields, enclosed in the 15th century, and the village, manor house and church were in their current positions, although only the church looks anything like it did in medieval times. The manor house (to the north of the church) and all the cottages were rebuilt from the 17th century onwards. The owner of

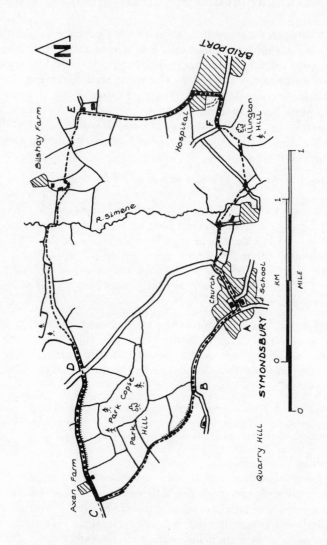

the deer park was almost certainly the main local landowner, but by the time of its single occurrence in the documentary record, in 1356, the park belonged to the Abbot of Cerne. Our road leads through houses and cottages of the local orange stone. Towards the top, on the left, one house has a simple but massive wooden door and surround dating from the 17th century, a rare survival. *Ignore turns to left and right, keeping on up the road, which turns into a gravel lane, deeply cut down* and with ferns in the banks. The trees arching overhead turn it into a tunnel. Occasionally outcrops of stone can be seen in the banks. The hedge on the right was part of the boundary of the deer park (now inhabited by cows), which can be glimpsed through a gate. *Keep on along the hollow way to a junction at the top of the rise* (B). *Take the right hand path into the fields along the hedgerow, downhill for a little way and then uphill again.* Away to the left is an isolated thatched cottage, and the hill beyond it is Quarry Hill, used from medieval times for stone. Even at this distance the irregular disturbances caused by the quarrying are clear.

The hedge to the right of our route is the boundary of the deer park – peer through the hedge to see the steep slope on the other side. The bank was designed to keep the deer in, and probably had a wooden paling on top of the bank: deer can jump great heights. Many deer parks had deer-leaps, which allowed deer to enter but prevented them leaving, thus increasing the herd. Symondsbury may have had one, but there is no evidence. The park is only 160 acres so hunting here would have been on foot, not horseback. Usually 2 deer were kept for each acre, so Symondsbury perhaps had 320 deer.

Keep on along the hedge to the top of the hill. The names here – this is Park Hill, and the wood in the valley below is Park Copse – led researchers to rediscover the deer park in the 1960s. When they examined the area they discovered the bank we have been following, and a document of 1356 which mentions a park at Symondesbergh 'in which there are no deer'. From the top of the hill is a good view of the undulating interior of the park, which would have had a mixture of grass and woods in medieval times. Much of it is still grazing, but parts are arable. The two streams inside provided water for the deer. The bank has been obliterated at the top of the hill, but continues down the other side. Good view looking south (seawards) with Quarry Hill on the right and the conical Colmers Hill (with its topping of conifers) left. Views open up to the north as well.

Go over the stile to keep straight on along the hedge, going downhill. The hedge is on a prominent bank again. Down in the valley to the right is Park Copse, mixed conifers and broad-leaved trees. *At the bottom of the hill go over the stile onto the fenced sandy track which goes uphill, still following the hedge line. At the top of the hill go through the metal gate* (C) *and the track turns rightish towards the farm.* The ash trees on the right were layered many years ago as part of a laid hedge, but have grown out to form trees.

Turn sharp right to go along the track to the farm and keep on past the farm buildings along the gravel road. The hedge on the right hand side is the boundary of the deer park, with a steep drop on the other side. The town of Bridport is visible in the far valley to the left. *Keep on the road, which goes down a short hill and joins a minor road.* (D) [Shortened route diverges here, and turns right down the road to return to Symondsbury. The road winds around and has several deep parts, with trees arching over the road. The road marks the other boundary of the deer park. Just as the road turns sharply right it crosses the little River Simene, by little industrial buildings. Rejoin main route here.] *The main route crosses the road and takes the grassy track between two hedges straight ahead, waymarked 'The Monach's Way' (which follows Charles II's many routes after escaping from the Battle of Worcester, 1651).*

A clear wide grassy path continues down the hill, through little fields of flowery unimproved grassland bordered by thick hedges. A spring on the left, one of many which emerge in the area. *The path goes over a little hill, and on down again to the right and then on along the path.* Furze here. *At the bottom of the hill bear right on the path leading to a Victorian metal gate. Go through the gate into open fields and then left along the hedge. At the far corner of the field turn right along the little River Simene. Walk a little way to a wooden gate with a bridge over the river. Go through the gate (waymarked), over the bridge, and take the path uphill straight on, leading towards a stone and thatch farmhouse on the top of the hill. As you reach the farm, bear right to a stile at the end of a post and rail fence. Go over the stile, and follow the sunken path (a modern ha-ha) round along an iron fence to another stile.* Bilshay Farm is partly 17th century, of stone with some brick, and is typical of many isolated farm settlements in this area. Unlike Axen Farm which we passed through earlier, Bilshay has old buildings and may be on the site of a medieval farm. Bilshay is in Allington parish: although today Allington seems just a suburb of Bridport, it was a separate village in medieval times.

Go over the stile, into open fields, and head diagonally right across the field towards the gate in the far right corner. Go through the metal gate, and head left across this field towards the white cottage (E). Follow hedgerow on left to cottage, don't take path through cottage garden, but turn right and walk along hedge. Go through gateway in the hedge to the next field, and on along the hedge line. This leads into a path with hedges either side, which gets more enclosed, with trees arching over it, goes downhill, and turns right becoming a ferny sunken track, emerging at the entrance to Bridport Hospital. Cross the road and turn right up the track. Here it is more like a lane, with a proper stone surface, like medieval roads. Trees arch overhead. *At the first bend (F) turn left into woods owned by the Woodland Trust, go up the path 50 yards and turn right along the side path. This contours along inside the wood. As it turns uphill, take the path branching off to the right, downhill.*

Symondsbury Church

Follow this path downhill, to the left, through an unusual modern metal stile and out into open fields. Walk downhill diagonally across the field to the gated track. This little valley of the River Simene has many trees – good stand of willows to the left, and poplars straight ahead. *When you reach the track, take the gate to the right and walk parallel to the little river towards the poplars and cottage. Cross the river at an inconspicuous concrete bridge, and turn right across the small field to cross a stile at the far (right) end. Cross the track and over the stile opposite into a field. Walk along the river, and over yet another stile to the next paddock. Half right towards the corner of the field to another stile, and a path leads on beside the river into a yard with small industrial buildings. Turn right just before the road, across a bridge on the river.* The complex of walls above the bridge was Symondsbury Sheepwash, a picturesque spot in Victorian times, admired in several Guide books.

[The shortened route rejoins here]. *Turn left up the road to Symondsbury which passes through a 25ft (8m) deep cutting.* On the edge of the village are farms, one with a stone and thatch barn on the roadside (right) and an even bigger one behind in the yard. The most substantial medieval farmyards would have looked like this, but mostly they would have been considerably poorer and smaller. Until Symondsbury's open fields were enclosed in the 15th century, virtually all the farms would have been in the village.

The church is on the right: there has been a church here since early medieval times, but the earliest surviving part is the central tower and the two transepts which are 14th century. Some of the other walls are late medieval, but most of the windows are modern, dating from a restoration of 1923. The basic layout of Symondsbury village is medieval, with the farms and cottages clustering around the church, but all the cottages are 17th and 18th century replacements.

Hambledon Hill and the Clubmen's Last Stand

A 4½ mile (7km) walk to Hambledon Hill, with one steady ascent, and one steadyish descent: 700ft (215m) of climbing over the whole walk. A shortened version (3½ mile, 5½km) can be walked. Wonderful views: a very varied walk with good downland on Hambledon. Well marked paths, usually dry because most of it is on chalk.

Introduction: In 1645, after three years of Civil War, the Clubmen rose in southern England and opposed both sides. They were mostly from the lower classes, and were fed up with the chaos of war, and in particular with being plundered by the armies of both sides. Their banners were inscribed 'If you offer to plunder or take our cattle, Be assured we will bid you battle'. The name came from their lack of weapons – most only had clubs. They made their final stand inside the old earthwork of Hambledon Hill.

Parking and Public Transport: Drive to Iwerne Courtney (sometimes called Shroton) and park in the lay-by opposite the church (A on the map ST860124). Possible to get here by bus from Shaftesbury, Bournemouth or Poole, but the more frequent service is from Blandford.

Information: Pub in Iwerne Courtney, close to the end (or start) of the walk.

Directions:
Facing the church, head to the right up the village street. Most of the cottages are brick, and date from after the Civil War, but the wall to the street of the pair of brick cottages just after Fairfield Road is of hard chalk, and has a 17th-century moulding over the window. The green on the right is called The Glebe, meaning land which belonged to the Rector, and farmed by him to make part of his income. Doubtless in the 17th century this was grazing being used by the Rector. Although the brick and rendered cottages only date back to the 18th century, this is where the 17th century village was – the cottages and farmhouses are replacements.
Turn left up the footpath marked 'General Woolfe's Close, going

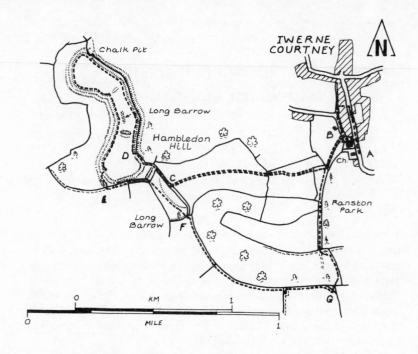

past the modern old people's housing, through the gate at the end, turning left onto a gravel track which joins a tarmac road. Keep left then keep straight on. Turn right into the fields over second stile by the cricket pitch (B) *with Public Bridleway sign. The path joins a chalky track leading uphill.* The Iron Age hillfort of Hambledon Hill can be glimpsed on the skyline right.

The wall to the left, prettily constructed from a mixture of stone, chalk, flint, stone tiles and red clay tiles, is the boundary of part of Ranston park, one of the big houses south of Iwerne Courtney. The wall probably dates from the 18th century.

Go through the metal gate, and turn right along the track leading uphill. Go through another metal gate, and on up the track. The fields on either side are arable now: in the 17th century they would have been grassy downland. This was probably the line of the route taken by Cromwell when his army brought the defeated Clubmen down to pen them in the church.

Three-quarters of the way up the hill gives a wide view back across the village, with the spire of Iwerne Minster church further up the valley. The isolated farms outside the village were probably already there by the time of the Civil War: Iwerne Courtney's medieval open fields were enclosed in 1548, allowing farms to be constructed in the fields. Before enclosure they would all have been in the village.

Carry on up the track through another gate. This fence line contouring around the slope is on a slight Neolithic earthwork, which relates to an enclosure higher on the hill.

Near the summit the impressive Iron Age earthworks of Hambledon Hill come into view on the right. *At the Ordnance Survey pillar (C) turn right towards Hambledon Hill along the path between the two fences.* Huge view from here, with the Blackmore Vale opening up to the north, and a big chalk pit on the hill opposite.

Go through the gate into the National Nature Reserve of Hambledon Hill (large sign), established because of the huge area of rich downland flora which has some scarce plants and many butterflies. The short flowery grass here, the true downland, would have looked just like this in the 17th century, but would then have covered an even larger area.

The earthworks just inside the Nature Reserve are outworks, extra banks to defend this more vulnerable side of the Iron Age fort. *Walk straight on along the path to the right of the banks* and one of the Iron Age entrances (D) appears in the main ramparts.

On 4th August 1645 Cromwell and his army had dispersed a large gathering of Clubmen near Shaftesbury by persuasion, assuring them that they would not be plundered. Cromwell came south to Hambledon Hill, where nearly two thousand Clubmen 'were drawn into one of the old camps upon a very high hill'. The Clubmen refused to parley with Cromwell, and fired on his soldiers, killing two of them and four horses from the group who tried to force their way through the entrance. Probably it was the entrance in front of us which the Clubmen defended. The Roundheads regrouped, and some of the attacking soldiers got behind the Clubmen, killed a dozen of them, injured many more and captured 300 prisoners. The rest ran away, leaving most of their arms. Cromwell recorded all this in a letter he wrote next day.

[Shortened walk: walk straight across the entrance through the interior of the hillfort to the ramparts on the far side, and rejoin the walk at E].

Go through the entrance, turn slightly right and follow the path to the top of the inner (highest) rampart of the hillfort. We shall walk almost around the hillfort on this inner rampart (nearly 1½ miles, 2km). Hambledon is the most impressive Iron Age hillfort anywhere, with huge ditches and banks. The Clubmen used it as a rendezvous because it was a large open space, well-defended by the ancient ramparts – the hillforts were deserted after the Romans invaded Britain, but many of them were sporadically used for meetings, like those of the Clubmen, which needed a large, neutral space. On the skyline on the left (in the middle of the fort) is a Neolithic long barrow, pre-dating the hillfort. After defeating the Clubmen, Cromwell's army spent the night in the hillfort after penning the prisoners in Shroton church. Wide view of the Blackmore Vale from the ramparts. *Follow the rampart when it turns down hill a little –* at the far corner is another Iron Age entrance, very steep and very cut about by a chalk pit.

Continue on the top of the inner rampart. The village of Child Okeford comes into view in the valley below. The rampart turns the corner, and a short very steep slope leads back up towards the summit of the hill. The ramparts then turn sharply right. The slight bank and ditch running across the hillfort marks its original size – the part we are now walking is an extension. These ramparts enclose the whole of the top of the chalk spur. Good view of the ramparts and the steep slope below, all still covered in downland turf. The little ridges running across them are terracettes, formed naturally. From this side the Neolithic long barrow shows clearly the gap cut through it – it is not known when this was done.

Shortly after passing the end of the long barrow (skyline left) follow the inner rampart to the right to reach another original entrance to the hillfort – possibly the Cromwellian cavalry used this entrance to come up behind the Clubmen who were defending the entrance on the far side.

Walk downhill through the entrance, (a smallish gap in the ramparts) and bear left to pass between the outer banks and then half right to the gate in the wire fence half right (E). Through gate and turn left onto a track, running uphill along the fence line. Through the metal gate, and on uphill on the now fenced track which emerges into an open grassy area. Head towards the slight bank on the crest of the hill slightly to the right.

This bank is part of a Neolithic ditch and bank (a causewayed camp) which surrounded the top of the hill, with outer defences further down like the one we passed on the way up the first hill. These have recently been excavated and form part of a complicated series of Neolithic monuments in this small area, which includes two Neolithic long barrows.

Walk straight on towards the track which turns along the ridge and slightly downhill. The low mound at right angles to the fence is one of the Neolithic barrows, and the bank running parallel to the fence is Neolithic too, an outwork to the enclosure on the hill top.

Go over the stile and on to the track. Carry on down the track, through a gate. (F) Hod Hill is clear on the right, another Iron Age hillfort .

Go through the second gate by the corrugated iron barn, and continue on the footpath straight down the hedge on the left, ignoring the track to the right. Straight ahead (or slightly right) the tops of the roofs of Stepleton House can be seen in the trees, surrounded by its well-treed park. The main part of the house dates from just before the Civil War, and parts of the park are probably of that date too.

Turn left through the gate at the bottom of the field (G) *along the path through the trees. Through another gate, and the path continues along at the bottom of a little steep down.* On the right is overgrown hazel coppice: at the time of the Civil War (and indeed for long before and after) hazel coppices were regularly cropped for thin timber to make hurdles, timber for thatched roofs and many other purposes.

The path joins a chalky track: turn right along the track, and straight on at the crossing of tracks immediately afterward. On the right is a thin belt of woodland bounded by an iron fence. *Continue along the track.*

This part of the walk gives the best idea of the 17th century landscape – most 17th century roads would have looked like the rough chalky track here, and the downs above the deserted valley would probably have had belts of woodland below, as they do here. The valley floor would probably have been pasture, rather than arable as it is now, and fences would not have been of wire, but overall the downs, woods and track give an impression of an earlier landscape.

Continue along the track, which rejoins our outward route at a metal gate. Continue downhill toward the cricket pavilion. Go over the stile (B), *turn right up the road, which turns left by a farmyard full of thatched buildings.* Although mostly dating from the 18th century, this yard gives a good idea of earlier farmyards – 17th century farms here would have had simple thatched and stone buildings just like these.

Turn right at the road junction and the car park comes into sight. The block of three stone cottages on the edge of the graveyard have been altered but are basically 17th century, with typical triangular gables in the front. They were probably originally thatched, and give a good idea of what the more substantial village cottages looked like at the time of the Civil War.

Shroton Church

Go up the church path. On the right, above the path, is a stone table tomb to Agnes Mew who died in 1670, aged 68 – she would have been 43 when the Clubmen were defeated, and must have witnessed the event.

Iwerne Courtney church was nearly new when the 300 Clubmen prisoners were herded into it – Sir Thomas Freke, the main local land-owner, had rebuilt it all (except the tower) in 1610, a very unusual date for church building. The building style is basically that of fifty years earlier, but the screen still to be seen inside is very up-to-date, with classical detailing. This is the only fitting surviving which was in the church in 1645 and now surrounds the chapel with its huge memorial to Sir Thomas Freke. The memorial dates from 1654. Hanging high on the wall opposite is a helm, an armoured headpiece dating from about 1560, but the added neckpiece dates from the Civil War, and is of the style worn by Cromwell's army. A few grave slabs by the pulpit mark the graves of people who were alive during the Clubmen's revolt. There are no gravestones to those who died in the battle: nor are they in the parish register, which only has five burials for all of 1645. They may have been buried back up on Hambledon Hill.

After a night in the church, the Clubmen's names were taken, they promised to revolt no more, and they were released. Cromwell, in the letter written that day, called them 'poor silly creatures', but retained their leaders for trial. Some managed to escape later, but seventeen were imprisoned at Sherborne, including several clergymen. The Clubmen's Revolt died out after the defeat of Hambledon Hill, and the Civil War ended less than a year later.

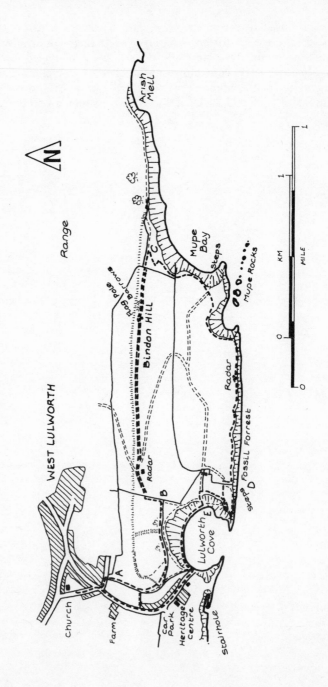

WEST LULWORTH

Range

Arish Mell

Bindon Hill

Bog pole Barrows

Mupe Bay

Steps

Mupe Rocks

Radar

Radar

Steps

Fossil Forrest

Lulworth Cove

Church

Farm

Car Park

Heritage centre

Stairhole

A

B

C

D

E

N

KM

MILE

Lulworth and Smuggling

Lulworth Cove and Bindon Hill are some of the finest parts of the Dorset coast. This walk gives the easiest route up Bindon Hill, but cannot avoid a steep descent. Part of the walk is inside the Army Ranges, open most weekends and school holidays (phone the Army to check: (01929 462721 extn 4819). The shorter route given as an alternative is always open, but it too has one very steep descent. The longer route is 4 miles (7km) the shorter 2 miles (3km), with 725ft (220m) of climbing.

Introduction: Smuggling was widespread all along the Dorset coast in the 18th and early 19th centuries: high duties on tea, tobacco, brandy, wine and many other goods made it a profitable trade which had support from all levels of society. By 1787 1,425 items paid high duties if imported, and smugglers could supply many things half price. Little of the huge quantity of tea drunk in England in the later 18th century paid duty – it was virtually all smuggled in. The Victorians made smuggling romantic, but the reality was much more brutal and business-like. Many of the goods smuggled came from the Channel Islands, and some from France. Purbeck had many secret bays suitable for the trade.

Parking and Public Transport: Drive to West Lulworth, and park on the side of the road on the hill leading down from the church (the road from Winfrith Newburgh SY823806). If there is no space here, drive down towards Lulworth Cove and use the big car park (fee). Walk back up the road to join the walk. Buses to Lulworth Cove from Wool Railway Station or Wareham, and less frequently from Dorchester.

Information: Lavatories, many pubs, cafes and so on in the part of Lulworth down by the Cove, and more in the village of West Lulworth. Small display on the area on the road up from the Cove, and a much larger one (including smuggling) at the Lulworth Cove Heritage Centre (by the car-park, and free with a car-park ticket, fee otherwise). Open daily, 9.30 am-6 pm in summer: winter hours shorter (01929 400587). Mupe Bay is good for swimming if the weather is warm enough.

Directions:

Walk down the hill, turn right at the T-junction and after 30 yards turn left into Bindon Road, a gravel track. Ignore turning to left (Sunnyside). Soon afterwards go over the stile on the right (A) (signed Lulworth Cove/Range walks). Take the path straight ahead keeping the hedge on your right. At a post indicating the path to Durdle Door, take the higher path (left) contouring round the slope.

All this area has superb downland flowers, at their best in June, but good all summer. Bee orchids are sometimes to be found, at intervals, all along this walk.

The path rises more steeply again, and Lulworth Cove comes into view. Customs officers often co-operated with smugglers and became rich. Others tried to do their duty and suffered for it. Two customs officers were roped together here and slung over the cliff, and only hauled back up after the smugglers had disposed of their goods. The gravestone of another officer who was killed by being thrown over the cliff at Durdle Door (just to the west) in 1832, still survives at Weymouth. *The path joins the lower path at a stile (don't go over stile). Bear left up the hill, keeping the fence on the right, and follow this path along the top of the cliff at the back of Lulworth Cove.*

A big bank and ditch runs at right angles to the cliff, back across Bindon Hill, one of several Iron Age earthworks which enclose the whole top of the hill. Superb views from here. *The path reaches a fence running at right angles to our path (B). This is the boundary of the Army Ranges.* [For a shorter route take the steep path down to the right until Lulworth Cove is reached and then the path up the far side to Pepler's Point, the eastern side of the entrance to the Cove]. *The main route goes left, steeply uphill along the fence to the top of the slope. Entrance on the right to the Army Ranges. Red flags fly and the gate is locked if the range is in use (the shorter route described above is always open). Go through the range gate, take the path straight ahead to the little Radar building. Straight across to the gravel track after the building, 35 yards on take the left hand track with a stone marked 'Bindon Hill Walk'.*

Lulworth Army Camp is visible in the valley to the left. Rough tracks like these were used by the smugglers to move their goods inland. In 1718 the Weymouth customs officer complained to London that smugglers 'come very often in gangs of 60 to 100 men to the shoar, in disguise armed with swords, pistolls, blunderbusses, carbines and quarter staffs' to carry off their goods. They not only defied the customs officers, 'but beat, knock down and abuse whoever they meet in their way'. Heathland like that surviving in the Army land below was a popular area for smugglers too.

Continue along the track, past the flag pole and beacon. Two Bronze Age round barrows to the left, on the crest of the hill. The towers of Lulworth Castle are visible set in trees inland to the left. Lights in the Castle windows were supposed to have signalled to smugglers landing at Arish Mell to let them know whether the coast was clear. Certainly landowners were often sympathetic to the smugglers, or even involved with the trade themselves.

In 1719 Lulworth Castle and 'other suspect houses' in East and West Lulworth were searched for smuggled goods, and 4 gallons of brandy were seized from one cottage. Mr Weld of the Castle claimed that two casks of wine found on the shore in 1716 were really his.

Stone cairn on the right, a memorial to men of the Royal Armoured Corps whose ashes were scattered in the area. A seat gives good views of Mupe Rocks down below, and left along the Purbeck coast.

Go on along the track, over stile in the fence, and the gravelled track fades out, becoming a grassy path. A seat on the right gives a rest in a good position for views. Just beyond, on the right is the steep path down, marked 'Mupe Beach and Coast Path'. (C)

Old boathouses, Lulworth Cove

[It is possible to continue eastwards along the coast path to Arish Mell, but the ground is rather broken and the path steep. If this addition is taken, return the same way to rejoin main route]

After admiring the view, take the steep path down to Mupe Bay. Despite being downhill, this is the stiffest part of the walk. Follow the path just inland from the cliff edge. Huge chalk landslips on the cliff, with the little inlet for Arish Mell beyond. This remote bay was often used by smugglers. In June 1777 'a Dunkirk schooner landed near Arish Mills (mell) upwards of twenty tons of tea', in defiance of the customs men on the cliff who were covered by the schooner's huge guns. Twelve hundredweight were seized by the customs, and taken to a pub in West Lulworth, but the well-armed smugglers followed, broke into the pub, injured the inhabitants and rescued their tea.

Worbarrow Bay, just beyond Arish Mell was the scene of open defiance by smugglers in October 1719 – 'five vessels runned their goods, there being a perfect fair at the waterside, as many in number as might be usually at Dorchester Fair'.

Mupe Bay was another of the many landing-spots for smugglers, who used a cave in the cliffs just to the west for storage, still called Smugglers Cave on the maps. [Steps lead down to the shore at Mupe Bay. Lots of trees. Return the same way].

Don't take gravelled road, but continue on the path along the cliff marked Coast Path to Lulworth. A small concrete look-out probably dates from the Second World War, but the Radar installation a little further along is part of the Army Ranges.

Continue on the coast path along the cliff top. About 1/3 mile along ledges are seen in the cliff, with rounded masses of stone – the Fossil Forest. The fossils are lumps of algae which accumulated around trees some 135 million years ago. A little further on concrete steps give access to these ledges and the 'Forest'. (D)

A large cave halfway down the cliff here was used as a store by local smugglers, who were lowered by ropes from the cliff top to unload the boat or recover their goods. It has since fallen in.

Go through the gate in the Army Ranges fence, and take the path straight on to Pepler's Point, the limestone cliff forming one side of the entrance to Lulworth Cove. [The shorter walk rejoins here]. A memorial stone makes a good seat. Good view of the cove and the chalk cliff behind – the first part of the walk was along the top of the cliff. The gap in the limestone has allowed the sea to erode the softer chalk, forming the Cove.

The opposite side of the entrance to Lulworth Cove had a coastguard look-out until the 1950s – its remains can be seen in the cliff falls.

A rather steep path leads straight down to the Cove. Take this, or retrace the path a little way east and take the slightly less steep path through woods on the left. Turn left at the bottom of this path, and a short steep scramble leads to the shore of the Cove. (E)

The Cove and other parts of the sea were used to conceal smuggled goods, especially wine and brandy. The wooden tubs were thrown in the water, held down by weights and marked with a buoy like those used for lobster pots. In 1717 the Customs found 'a hogshead of French red wine moored with ropes to several stones' in Lulworth Cove, and confiscated it. Besides the usual tea, wine, brandy and tobacco, Lulworth dealt with some more specialised cargoes – expensive cocoa beans were smuggled through here in 1719, and sent straight on to London. The oddest smuggling tale was invented by Thomas Hardy, who wrote a short story describing how smugglers brought Napoleon Bonaparte (then at war with England) over to Lulworth to reconnoitre for a French invasion. Hardy was very amused when this became part of local folklore as a real happening.

Walk along the shore of the Cove, round to the road where fishermen's buildings meet the shore. The sea here is usually very cold because many freshwater springs emerge at the shore line.

Turn right up the road to the village. Small display (free) on the area in a wooden building beside the road. The long row of houses at right angles to the road were built in the 19th century as Coastguard cottages. The Coastguard, founded in 1822, worked with the Royal Navy to wipe out smuggling, which declined from 1815, and had virtually gone by 1850. Changes in the law, and the removal or reduction of duties from many commodities, helped the change. In 1822 smuggling was still going on in Dorset, as the Customs realised when brandy was offered for sale at 8s (40p) a gallon in Yeovil.

Continue up the road, past the spring-fed mill pond and the ornamental thatched cottages. The Lulworth Cove Heritage Centre (fee) has good displays on the area, including smuggling. *The road leads up the hill, back to where the car was parked.*

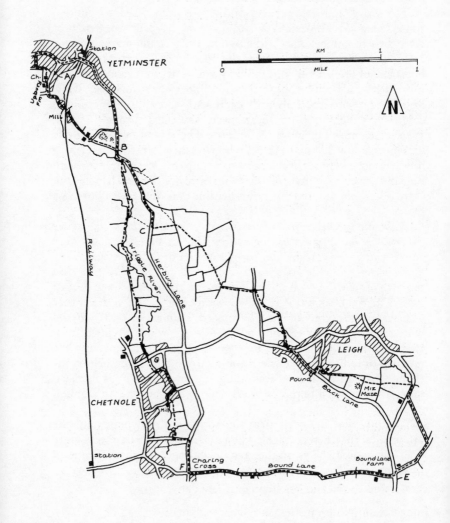

The Vale of the Little Dairies
Cows in the Blackmore Vale

A walk through the lush pastures of the Blackmore Vale. The footpaths all through the area are mostly well signed, with yellow arrows on little circular waymarks. The walks can be muddy, and boots are recommended. The undulations of the countryside (325ft, [100m] spread over the whole walk) make the views change all the time, and although the area is mostly grass, there are tall hedges and lots of trees. This is real working countryside. The walk starts in Yetminster, wanders across to Leigh, takes a deserted lane across to Chetnole and then follows the Wriggle River back up to Yetminster. The main route is 7¼ miles (12km), but a short cut provides an alternative of 5 miles (8km). If the train alternative is used the walk is 5¼ miles (8½km).

Introduction: 'Everywhere there are cows, for the smell of cows is the incense of North Dorset' (Sir Frederick Treves, *Highways and Byways in Dorset* [1906]). The Blackmore Vale, Hardy's Vale of the Little Dairies, has had rich pastures ever since it was cleared of forest. The clay subsoil and the wettish climate are ideal for grass. This walk gives a good sample of an area still dedicated to the cow, using the wide old droveways, and tracing the little River Wriggle. Halfway round is the curious Miz Maze, and everywhere there are cows.

Parking and Public Transport: Drive to Yetminster, and park in the wide back road by the church (A on map ST595107). The church is in the south-east part of the village. This walk is possible by public transport: take the train to Yetminster (Weymouth – Bristol route). You can return by train from Chetnole, but do check the times of the trains as they are not very frequent. Buses also run from Dorchester and Yeovil and less frequently from Sherborne.

Information: No lavatories on the route, but there are pubs in Yetminster (two, one by the station, one in the High Street), in Leigh (east of the church on the main road) and particularly usefully in the middle of Chetnole, two-thirds of the way around the walk.

Directions:

Yetminster has the largest number of 17th century and earlier stone cottages and farmhouses of any Dorset village. *Walk down Church Street away from the church towards the little triangle in the middle of the road.* Many good stone buildings here – Manor Farmhouse is a particularly fine example, dating from the late 17th century. Cross Farm still has its farm buildings behind. *Turn left up High Street,* which has many more handsome buildings – Manor House and Petty's Farmhouse are perhaps the best. New imitation local style cottages (Petty's Farm) on the right, thatched. The White Hart Inn is early 17th century. *Turn left up Queen Street, and left at the end of that road, along a tarmac path with hedges either side. Through the old kissing gate, along the path by the churchyard and right along the path to the church.* Look inside the church – built of the same local stone as the old cottages, and virtually all dating from around 1450. *Walk around the church tower if you haven't gone inside the church, or out of the door opposite the one you entered by if you did, and go through the wooden gate and up the path by the cottage.* As you reach the road look up to the right to see Upbury Farm, a late medieval farmhouse, with later alterations. Two blocked windows and the archway are original. On the wall opposite is a plaque recording Benjamin Jesty (1736-1816) who lived at Upbury Farm, and who pioneered the use of cowpox injections to inoculate people against smallpox. He fattened cattle here for the London market, and had noticed that milkmaids (who often caught cowpox from their charges) did not get the much more dangerous smallpox.

Turn right along the road, and at the bend 50 yds on turn left into Mill Lane, which runs downhill. Keep on down the road, past cottages, go over the river, and then over the railway (be careful of the trains). The road becomes a gravel track. On the right is Yetminster Mill, partly 17th century. The handsome outbuilding is dated 1833. *The track becomes a path, and continues uphill, past some wooden buildings, then over a concrete track. Go over the wooden stile opposite into fields, and on straight ahead.* The fields are small. In *Tess of the D'Urbervilles* Hardy contrasted the Blackmore Vale with the wide open high chalklands to the south. 'Here, in the valley, the world seems to be constructed upon a smaller scale: the fields are mere paddocks'. And so many of them are still.

Keep along with the hazel hedge on your right. Go through the metal gate (B), immediately right onto a track and through another gate. Ignore the bridge which comes up soon on the right, and continue along the path through this woody overgrown drove. The area has many of these droveways, presumably to make moving cattle about easy. Cattle were fed on Leigh Common until it was enclosed in 1804, and some of the droves lead there. Some are still open, some have developed into roads, and others, like this one, have virtually become woodland.

The path goes over a wooden bridge and through a metal gate. Keep straight on. This part is muddy in wet weather. Big hedgerows either side, with many different sorts of trees and shrubs. *The path turns right, and becomes more open with trimmed hedges. At the massive old oak (C) on the right, turn left (waymarked) through a metal gate into a field. Go straight across the field,* which is much larger than most around here, and has 'improved' grass designed to be cut as silage to provide winter feed for cattle. The farm visible on the left has a big silage tower for storage. In the 17th century, when we have evidence from inventories of people's possessions, herds of cows here were small, with most dairy herds consisting of only 7-10 cows. Cheese and butter were produced for sale – selling fresh milk further afield was impossible before the fast transport provided by the railways. In the 17th century beef cattle for meat were fattened in this area, as they still are.

The two gates together on the far side show where a hedge has been removed. *Go through one of them and turn right to go diagonally across the field to a stile visible in the right hand hedge. Go over this double stile,* into one of the few arable fields of the area. *Head for gap in the hedge by the water trough straight ahead, over another double stile, into another arable field, straight across the field to a gap in the hedge to the right of the iron gate, with a stile. Over this, left along the hedge a little way until next hedge is reached, turn right along the hedge to a ditch with plank bridge over. Cross the bridge and continue along the hedgeline to a stile which leads into a lane.* The area has always had a little arable: probably in medieval times in open fields which were enclosed before the early 17th century. By the time of the first surviving survey of the area (1614) 80% of the land was grass. By 1840 Leigh and Chetnole had an even greater area under grass. In the 18th and 19th centuries Dorset had an unusual method of letting dairies – the farmers rented the cows to a dairyman, charging a price per cow per year, but supplying the cows, land and feed. In 1812 many dairies had only 12-20 cows. Quantities of butter were sent to London.

In 1815 the agricultural writer Stevenson observed that the 'best servants' came from the families of the small dairy farmers in the Blackmore Vale 'who bring up their children in habits of sobriety, honesty and industry, and give them that small portion of education which is suited to their condition'.

Go straight over the lane and through the right-hand gate and then diagonally across the field to the bend in the hedge ahead. Walk along this hedge (i.e. hedge on your left) to the metal gate. Through gate and on along the hedge to corner of the field. Go over the stile on the right of the gate, past a big willow, over a plank bridge, across another stile and turn right across the small field to the gap between industrial buildings and new houses. Go up the path, and emerge at the road (D). Fudge's Bakery to the right is an old-established firm, now producing fine cakes and biscuits. This is Leigh, pronounced Lie. [To shorten the walk turn right along the road, which reaches a ford on the outskirts of Leigh in about a mile and rejoin the walk at G]. *For the main route, turn left along the road, and right at the next road junction, up Back Drove,* one of the droves which has developed into a road. Along up on the right is the Pound, probably built in 1695 and recently restored. The walled enclosure was used to 'pound' straying animals – their owners had to pay a fine to retrieve them.

Manor Farm, Yetminster

Turn left down the road opposite the pound, and then right up the tarmac lane marked No Through Road. The stone farmhouse on the left is a fine example and is dated 1792. The style is more like 17th century farmhouses than late Georgian buildings.

Turn right opposite the drive to the farmhouse into the field through a metal gate. Walk left along the fence, through a gate in a fence, on uphill along the hedge, over a combined gate/stile. Keep straight on across the next field to the gate opposite. Just before the gate, on the right, on the summit of the hill, is the Miz Maze, a hexagonal bank which originally enclosed a maze. The centre now has only a little mound. John Hutchins, the county historian, stated in 1774 that it had been used within living memory, 'the young men of the village' scouring out the trenches and paring the banks once every six or seven years. Mazes were frequent in medieval England, but few survive.

Superb wide views of the chalk ridge to the south from the vicinity of the Miz Maze. *Go on straight across the field, downhill to gate, through gate and on across the next field to another gate on the far side. Out onto the road, turn right and after 50 yards turn left into another drove* – this one open here. The area around the Miz Maze and these droves was Leigh Common until 1804, when it was enclosed. These droves were laid out then – this one was called Water Drove. *At the junction of droves, turn right down the wooded one, which emerges into the open again and turns slightly right. Turn left at the road (E) and then after 25 yards right down the side road to a farm.* This is Bound Lane, which runs to Chetnole. It is not the parish boundary, despite the name, but marked the line between two different farms.

Keep on along this lane which is shown on the 1804 map as Bound Lane Farm. The lane leads to Chetnole, becoming a gravel lane, and a bit overgrown in the middle, but still with a clear path through. The isolated trees in the fields mark old hedge lines. Many oaks along the path too. Hutchins in the 1770s remarked on the large numbers of oaks and elms in the area – all the elms have died of elm disease. With the coming of the railways milk could be transported to the big towns. Previously fresh milk sales were impossible at any distance because milk goes sour so quickly. Part of Hardy's 'Tess' describes the life of the milkmaids and men who hand-milked the cows out in the fields or in the farmyard – the method used from prehistoric times. *Eventually the lane meets a road at a junction sarcastically called Charing Cross (F).* [If you are returning by train, take the lane straight ahead, go right when you meet the road, and left soon afterwards. The station is a quarter of a mile (0.5km) along].

The main route turns right along the road, and then left through the second gateway (waymarked) on the left, down the side of the hedge, through a garden gate and past the cottage into a road. Turn right, after 20 yards, through a gate into a field, and continue straight ahead, passing old farm buildings on your right. Go over the stile (built into a gate) and keep straight ahead, with the little river on the left. Go through the metal gate, on across the next field and then over the stile straight ahead which leads into a garden-like area. Turn left to go over a stile in a stone wall. Chetnole Mill is on the left. The little Wriggle River we have been following seems too small in summer to provide power, but in fact it worked three mills – this one, the mill at Yetminster we saw earlier and another high up at Withybrook. The Wriggle runs northwards towards Somerset, and soon joins the River Yeo.

Turn right along the path by the river. This soon turns right to join a drive and then a road. Turn left down the road, and then left again when another road is reached. Go over the river, then over the stile on the right by the metal gate. (The centre of Chetnole is straight on down this road, with a pub and shop). *Go straight across the field to a gate on the far side, over the road (ford to right) and through the gate to the right of Fordmead Cottage (G)* (with fine 17th-century stone front), *across the yard, through a small wrought-iron gate, across garden and out over the stile in the corner. The path continues along the river (wooded here), and emerges over a stile into fields.* (If taking a right-of-way through a garden is too intimidating, go left along the road, turn right at the junction and first right up concrete road).

We now follow the footpath markings through the fields, mostly alongside the Wriggle River, and this leads us back to Yetminster. The route description sounds more complicated than it is on the ground. *Go straight across the field towards the big trees to the stile on the far side, over double stile and along the hedge on the left, through the gateway and then over the stile on the right. Turn half-left towards the remnants of a hedge and then walk along the hedgeline (keeping hedge on the left) over a double stile, across field and through a wide gap to the right of jutting out hedgerow and then over another double stile in far corner. Go across the field, keeping the Wriggle River on the right, through gate, then right over a stile and immediately left over another stile just before a bridge over the river.* The river is only visible from a distance because of the trees growing along it. Yetminster church is visible to the left.

The path leads through the field, keeping the river on the right, with wide places where the cattle drink. Big herds of cows wander over a wide area. *Keep along the river, heading for the stile straight ahead in the hedge. Go over, and over the bridge. Turn left and rejoin our outward route. The path turns right and goes through a metal gate (B). Take the path straight ahead uphill (leaving the outward route) between two hedges.* Good view to the right through a gate where the path joins a track. *Keep on uphill along the track. This joins a tarmac road, passes a limekiln on left and then goes downhill. Turn left at main road, and follow this road to the middle of Yetminster. It passes over the river and railway (pub by railway station) and back to the little triangle in the middle of the road. The car is parked in the road to the left, Church Street.*

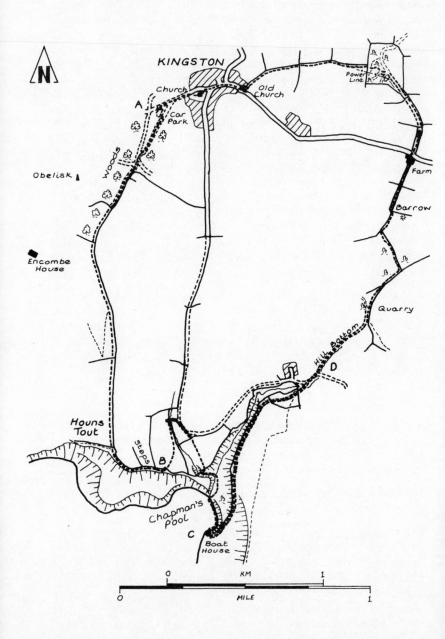

N

KINGSTON

Church

Old Church

Power Line

A

Car Park

Woods

Obelisk

Encombe House

Farm

Barrow

Quarry

Hill Bottom

D

Houns Tout

Steps

B

Chapman's Pool

C

Boat House

0   KM   1

0   MILE   1

Encombe – a Regency Estate

A walk from Kingston (the estate village) along the ridge overlooking Encombe to the sea, down Houns-tout Cliff to the bay at Chapman's Pool, and back along a secluded limestone valley to Kingston. The whole area is only accessible on foot, and is full of sheep, unimproved grassland, woods and scrub, all with lots of flowers, butterflies and birds. One very steep part down Houns-tout to the shore, but only an easy steady climb back up. The paths are well-marked (and the private drives even better indicated). Some of the paths beyond Houns-tout area rather rough, with lots of stones or over uneven ground. The main walk is 5½ miles (9km) with 525ft (160m) of climbing: a very short alternative is 3 miles (5km) and gives easy, flat access to one of the highest and remotest parts of the Dorset coast.

Introduction: The big estates in Dorset have had a huge effect on the landscape, particularly in the 18th and 19th centuries when their lands were ornamented with woods, parks and even artificial lakes. Estate villages were often rebuilt in Victorian times, and usually the church too. Kingston and Encombe show all these features, with the bonus of the big house being set in a remote and beautiful valley.

Parking and Public Transport: Drive to Kingston village, and turn into the village by the Scott Arms, into West Street. Continue straight through the village passing the church on your left and park in the car park signposted 'Car Park for Houns-Tout footpath 50 yards' just beyond the junction. (A on map SY953794). There are buses to Kingston from Wareham, Swanage and Poole.

Information: Pub in Kingston, and Nursery Tea Rooms (open summer weekends only) close to the start of the walk.

Directions:
All the narrow roads around the car park lead eventually to the big house of Encombe, and most of them are private with no public right of way. *Take the path leading from the back of the car park (by the noticeboard), which soon joins a gravel road. Turn right along this road, which is signposted 'Houns Tout'. Keep on along this road.* The woods we are passing through are part of the estate, which extended to 6,869 acres in 1871. The woods were partly for

profit and partly ornament.

After the road goes downhill a little, a complex junction of roads and paths is reached. Take the second left – a gravel track – with a finger post indicating 'Footpath to Houns Tout'. (To the left is the Nursery Tea Rooms). *Keep on along the track.* Mixed trees here, with some older beeches and ashes. *Go over the stile into open fields.* An astonishing view opens up, with the Encombe valley below, and the limestone ridge leading on ahead. On the opposite side of the valley is a tall stone obelisk, erected in 1835 to honour the brother of the Earl of Eldon.

Encombe belonged to the Pitt family in the 18th century, but most of the landscape features we see were the work of John Scott, later 1st Earl of Eldon, who bought the estate in 1807. He had a mile long tunnel pierced through the tree-covered ridge to our right to bring in water for the house, farms and for the ornamental lake in front of the big house.

All along this ridge are well-placed stone blocks for seats to admire the views. They were probably put here in the early 19th century.

Keep on along the path, beside a drystone wall, crossing a stile. The roof of the big house, with its brick-walled garden can be seen below, along with the lake. Lord Eldon was Lord Chancellor for 25 years, and had the great Seal of England at Encombe with him when fire broke out in the house in 1812. He 'secured it underground', but 'during the next day the family were occupied in digging for it, the Chancellor having forgotten the spot of its burial' (Hutchins). They eventually found it. Recollections of the estate in the early 20th century by R.E. Dorey include a footman rowing the children of the house on the lake, and a donkey boy who looked after the two donkeys kept to take the children out every day. Fifteen indoor servants included three footmen. Outdoors one of the carpenters spent all his time looking after the gates and fences, and a full-time blacksmith was also employed. Five gamekeepers waged war on the rabbits, and four men looked after the woods, supplying all the timber needed for building and fencing.

Ignore the ramp leading down to the right, continue along the ridge, over another stile. From the next stone block seat admire the view. Hutchins in 1774 found 'the valley and the southern slopes' consisting 'of pasture for sheep, yielding a greater plenty of grass and more beautiful verdure than is usually seen in the island [of Purbeck], and from its fertility it has been distinguished by the name of the "Golden Bowl"'. Still most of the land is pasture, with a ribbon of trees down the valley and bigger woods elsewhere. The farm below the lower lake was Encombe Dairy, which had a show dairyhouse in Victorian times. The lower lake had a summer house lined with moss early this century, round with five windows, much used by local courting couples when the family was away. The tallest part along the coast to the west is Swyre Head, with a very clear Bronze Age barrow on the ridge just inland. At Eldon's Seat, a knoll below it, is a stone seat where the first Lord Eldon's favourite dog is buried.

Go over another stile, with a 1980 stone seat with back just beyond. Wonderful coastal views, with the grey Kimmeridge Clay cliffs in the foreground. In the early 19th century salt water was pumped up to the house from here for the fashionable saltwater baths.

We are on top of Houns-tout, the end of the limestone ridge, and 500ft above the sea. *Bear left and along the path signed 'Chapman's Pool' between the edge of the cliff and a fence.* Good views (almost as from a plane) of the bay of Chapman's Pool and St Aldhelm's Head beyond. The top of the cliffs opposite has a clear band of limestone. Big 1976 landslip on one side, which closed the old coast path route.

The main route now goes down the steep face of Houns-tout, assisted by steps. This is the most severe part of the walk, and the shortened route simply turns back here and returns the way it has come. (Walk down to Kingston village from the car park to admire the church and village – see end of walk). If you can face the descent, our way back up is steady and not steep.

Keep on a little way along the cliff after the steps finish, and then follow the Coast Path stone markers by turning left over a stile, away from the cliff into the fields (B). This valley is also all pasture, scrub and woodland, with no arable. *Keep on across the field, heading for an earthen causeway running across the floor of the valley. Turn right over a stile and over the causeway,* which must be a relic from one of the carriage drives which Lord Eldon built around the estate. *Join a tarmac track and turn right along that road.* [Going left along this road up the valley could be used as a short-cut back to Kingston]. *Continue along the tarmac road until it ends, over the stile and on down the path towards Chapman's Pool. Go over another stile, and abruptly and steeply downhill. Turn left at the stone Coastal Path marker (To the Beach), on down the overgrown tiny valley.* The paths here are through landslips and alter frequently. At the bottom the path is rather wet. *Cross the stream and turn right towards the sea.* This path goes through a recent slip, and is humpy, with good flowers. *Keep wriggling along close to the stream, and the path reaches Chapman's Pool.* Impressive views to the right of Houns-tout, including the steep slope we came down. What looked like an undercliff right on the sea from on top is really only halfway down the cliff. The grey industrial looking cliffs are of Kimmeridge shale, and some of the slabs exposed on the beach show fossils of ammonites. The cliffs are very unstable: best to keep away from them.

The first Lord Eldon 'formed a very beautiful drive underneath the cliffs towards Chapman's Pool, but the soil, being of a shifting nature and full of springs, gave way' (Hutchins). This melodramatic landscape suited early 19th century taste well, and access by carriage would have made it perfect. Philip Brannon in his 1864 *Purbeck Guide* extolled 'the dark, heavy, laminated, and mouldering appearance of these cliffs' with sufficient 'variety of form to render them picturesque'! The boat house here was a lifeboat station 1860-80: it was replaced by one at Kimmeridge. *Walk along the shore with its odd chocolate-brown sand, or the cliff at high tide, to the little boat houses and hard* (C). *Take the rough track from behind the boat houses heading uphill and inland.*

The track keeps on steadily up the valley, which is more like a northern limestone dale than southern England. The very bottom is narrow and steep, mostly filled with trees. Lots of flowers, birds and butterflies in the wild grassland. *Go through a gate and on down the track, over a brick bridge and turn right on the tarmac road, signposted Renscombe.* The little settlement of Hill Bottom is up to the left. *Continue along the tarmac road for about 100 yards, and where the road starts to go uphill, turn left by a finger post signed Afflington Farm to go up a side valley* (D). We shall follow this valley for ½ mile. *The track follows the stream. Keep on up here,* partly through woodland. *Ignore the path to the right (to Worth), and when the track turns steeply up to the left, continue on the path straight ahead in the valley. Go through a metal gate and on again up the valley, through another metal gate and into open fields. On steeply up a little hill, and keep straight on with the stone wall on your left.* The big Bronze Age barrow on the right was partially excavated in the 1850s, but survives as an impressive mound. At the corner, look back to see the quarry half left. *Turn left at the corner, over the stile and then right along the path between two hedges.* Kingston church is visible to the left. *The path becomes a track. Keep on towards the farm buildings: the path passes between the cottages and converted barn.*

We come out onto the main road (it is possible to turn left back for Kingston, but the road is busy and has narrow verges). *Turn to*

The old pump and Kingston

the right and immediately left to take a track downhill. One of the best views of Corfe Castle straight ahead, sitting in the gap in the chalk ridge. *Keep on down the track, passing through two gates.* Good stone walls here, as there have been in many places along this walk.

After the second gate, continue along the track which goes on following the stone wall (right) for a little way and then emerges into open grazing with scrub on the left. The next bit is difficult, but the power line helps. Go past the pole where the power line makes a bend and past the pheasantry (both on left). Below the pheasantry turn left (E) leaving the main track to follow a wriggly grassy path through the scrub. Walk parallel to the power line, which is about 50 yards to your left. Ignore paths/tracks which run uphill and under the power line. When the path turns right to go more steeply downhill turn left onto a stoney path which tunnels through a thick hedge, across a stile and into open fields. (Difficult bit over).

Keep straight on after the stile, with the stone wall on your right. The tower of Kingston Old Church can be seen in front – we are heading for this. The path contours along, going slightly uphill. *Go through a gate and continue following along the wall. Turn uphill towards the church at the next gate (don't go through the gate), past the church and over stile into the main road. Turn right down the road.* The 'old' church, now a house, was built in 1833 by the first Earl of Eldon, in rather fanciful early Gothic revival style.

The best view of the new church which replaced it is from just above the pub. On the left is the school and schoolhouse, built by the estate in 1856. On the right is a typical estate cottage, all of stone and called 'Foreman's Cottage'. Kelly's *Directory* records that the whole village was 'almost entirely rebuilt within the years 1855-95', and most of the neat stone cottages, some still with latticed windows, survive. They all belonged to the estate, and up to the First World War roses were supplied by the estate to be planted in the gardens. Virtually everyone in the village worked for the estate, and no-one except shepherds and cowmen was allowed to keep a dog. Early in the 20th century the craftsmen on the estate were allowed to wear a frock coat and top hat on Sundays to distinguish their rank.

Walk straight on, past the pub and then up the path to the church. We pass the solid-looking village pump, which had 78ft of rods beneath it to reach the water. The new church, completed in 1880, is a very fine example of Victorian Gothic, impressive and austere externally, but with a complex plan. Designed in 'Early English' style by the well-known architect G.E. Street, it is an oddly massive church for a small village. All the stone is local, quarried on the estate, and the oak for the roofs and the stone slates came from Eldon lands in Gloucestershire. Worth seeing inside for the fine original ironwork, designed by the architect, and the stained glass.

Take the path to the left through the trees from the church, and return to car park.

Portland – Quarries and Convicts

Portland is very distinctive – physically separate from the rest of Dorset, and a completely stony landscape. This 5½ mile (8km) walk takes in the best of the island, and gives wonderful sea views. The route has only a little uphill work (200ft, 80m) and that easy. The walk goes up one side of the island, across its width and back down the other side. Wide views and many quarries. The paths are easy to find and usually dry. Good flowers on much of the route.

Introduction: Portland Stone is the finest English building stone, hard and almost white, with a very even texture. Like all limestones it was formed from sediments deposited in water, in this case a sea, something like 150 million years ago, and transformed into hard stone. Seaside shells and so on can be seen as fossils in some beds, especially one particular bed called the Roach.

The Romans quarried the stone, but it was mostly only used locally until the 17th century because it was very hard for medieval tools to work it, and because so much overburden had to be removed before the good stone was reached. Sir Christopher Wren used huge quantities of Portland Stone for the rebuilding of London after the Great Fire of 1666, and from then onwards it was fashionable and quarries expanded.

Parking and Public Transport: Follow the road signs on Portland for the Museum and Church Ope Cove, and park in the large car park signed 'Museum, Church Ope' at the lower end of Wakeham. (A on map SY695711). Buses regularly from Weymouth to Portland – Easton Square is the nearest stop, but Portland Heights may be possible.

Information: Cafe at Church Ope Cove, Portland Heights Hotel just off the route halfway round, pubs at Wakeham and Reforne. Public lavatories at Portland Heights (Yeates Road, top of Old Hill). Portland Museum open daily 10.30 am-1 pm, 1.30-5pm. Easter to September, shorter hours in winter, but open weekends (01305 821804).

Directions:
Cross the road, heading left to Portland Museum (well worth visiting: very good on Portland's history and quarrying). The arch

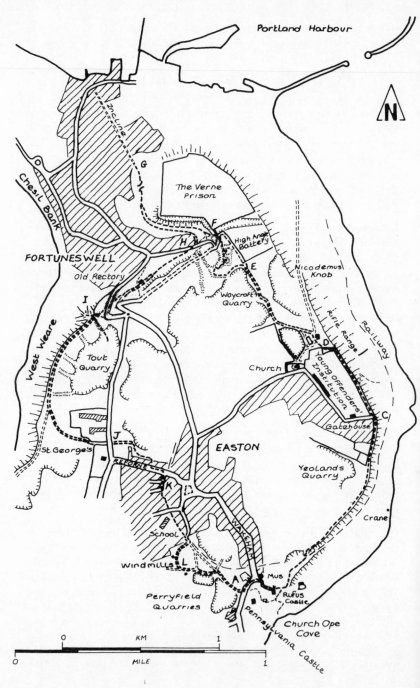

Portland Harbour

N

Incline

Chesil Bank

G

The Verne Prison

F

FORTUNESWELL

High Angle Battery

H

E

Old Rectory

Waycroft Quarry

Nicodemus Knob

Rifle Range

Railway

I

West Weare

Tout Quarry

Church

D

C

Young Offenders Institution

Gatehouse

C

St. George's

J

REFORNE

EASTON

Yeolands Quarry

Crane

K

WAKEN

School

Windmills

L

A

Mus

B

Rufus Castle

Perryfield Quarries

Pennsylvania Castle

Church Ope Cove

0   KM   1

0   MILE   1

opposite the Museum was one of the entrances to Pennsylvania Castle, and the low building inside was one of the lodges (see end of walk). The museum has fossil wood from the stone quarries outside, and incorporates one of the few surviving 17th-century Portland Stone cottages.

Go right into Church Ope Road and on down path beside the museum, past the cafe, and through the metal gate. The walls and cottages are all of Portland Stone, some of the walls being of very thin slabs. Rufus Castle, on the right of the path beyond the gate, is a neat triangular, late medieval building perched on a rock outcrop. Not accessible. The 19th century access bridge crosses the path. *Just beyond is a good viewpoint with seats* (B), and below is Church Ope Cove. Stone was transported from a quay here in the 18th century, and the overgrown cliffs were used as a dumping place for the overburden which had to be removed before the good stone could be quarried. [Signposts point the way to the ruins of the medieval church of St Andrew. Steep path down and then up to the ruins. Return to your starting point if you take this strenuous diversion].

Take the little signed path leading uphill to the left to the top of the cliffs. Take the clear path which continues through the old quarries, along a track, and then by a zig-zag uphill to the very top of the cliff. We are heading north along the cliff.

The quarries here are typical of Portland: rather bleak, with blocks of stone all over the place, dumps of overburden, and a general feeling that the whole surface of the earth has been moved. Very unnatural, and very chaotic. Good wild plants, including orchids, survive amongst the chaos. The cliff shows the horizontal stone beds clearly.

Until about 1800 all the Portland Stone quarries were on the edge of the cliffs because it was easier to quarry the stone there and let it tumble to the shore, rather than having to extract it from deep quarries inland, where 10-50 ft of overburden would have to have been removed.

The top of the cliffs gives a good view back over the southern tip of Portland, with two of the lighthouses just visible. *Continue on the upper path along the cliff edge parallel to the track.* Further along part of the iron fence on the seaward side of the path is of rails from a light railway used by the quarries. The Easton and Church Ope railway, which opened in 1902, ran through the under-cliff below. Inland is an overgrown quarry.

Keep along the clifftop path which joins a track. A little further along on the inland side is one of the deepest stone quarries, Yeoland Quarries, partly overgrown, but partly in use. On the shore, a few fishermen's huts and a crane for lifting the boats into the sea marks the site of one of the piers used for exporting stone.

The huge stone buildings of the Young Offenders' Institution are clear on the clifftop ahead: we are walking towards them. *Keep along the cliff path towards a little redbrick building of the Second World War. The path is enclosed by walls here with a vertical cliff on the seaward side.* The huge Portland stone buildings of the Young Offenders' Institution on the left are early 20th century, on the site of the Prison built from 1848 to house the convicts brought here to build Portland Harbour.

The path joins one of the roads in the Young Offenders' Institution, keep straight ahead. (C) [Alternative route – the road inland leads up to the original Prison buildings. The 1848 gatehouse, 1850 row of terraced houses, school and church of 1870, are all of Portland Stone and in Norman style. Walk round the church, across the grassy plot and through wall on right to rejoin main route].

Good viewpoint up a few steps on the right by the road junction, with the wide sweep of Weymouth Bay and along the coast to Purbeck. Portland Harbour is just coming into view directly northwards. This was built from 1846 as a refuge for shipping, much needed because storms and violent seas caused many wrecks here. Portland Stone was used for the huge breakwaters, and prisoners for the labour. *The road continues along the clifftop, with the wall of the Young Offenders' Institution alongside. The road is marked Private, but it is a footpath.* Below the cliff is a huge buttressed stone wall, part of a rifle range. Grove Farm, on the left, has big plain stone buildings. *Keep on along the road until a high stone wall makes the road turn inland. Follow the wall and then turn right through a gap in the wall out into open land* (D) *keep straight ahead to the tarmac road.* The Norman style church of 1870 is just visible to the left [alternative route rejoins here].

The small but heavy stone buildings (right) were engine houses for the railway which carried the stone quarried by the convicts to the Harbour. The steep road running down the hill was the railway incline of 1842. Worth walking to the viewpoint on the cliff edge for the wider view.

Turn left into a gravel track marked MOD property, (the gravel track is blocked with great lumps of stone). Peek over the high wall on the left of the track to see the most unusual playing ground, constructed in 1930s – right at the bottom of a deep quarry. In the distance a stack of stone, called Nichodemus Knob, shows the old ground surface. The stack was preserved as a navigation mark and shows the amount of quarrying which has gone on here.

Continue along the gravel track, turning right at the first junction by piles of stone. The track passes entrances to Waycroft Quarry, still in use. *Keep on along the track and turn left at the iron gate by the fenced enclosure* (E) *and follow the base of the bank. This becomes a worn path. Turn right where steps lead up the bank by another entrance to Waycroft Quarry.* The path is the track of one of the railways, built in the later 19th century to carry stone. Some of the stone sleepers which supported the rails can still be seen. *After 65 yards along the old railway line, turn right, in front of a big bank into High Angle Batteries,* built as an extra defence to the Verne (see below) in 1892, and used in the Second World War. *Sharp right inside the earthworks, down concrete steps into the gun battery.* The well preserved concrete tunnels, dated 1892, are ammunition stores for the emplacements. *Carry on along the wide pathway in the bottom, turning left and on past three blockhouses. Keep on the pathway which soon emerges at a car park at the entrance to the Verne* (F).

The stone entrance to the Verne is dated 1881. This huge fort was constructed from 1860 for the Army, and converted to a prison in 1948. The huge stone-lined ditches were one of the quarries for Portland Harbour, and the whole of the hillsides around were adapted as defensive earthworks, with the outer areas smoothed to give a clear range of fire for the guns.

Walk up to the bridge, and take the steep path to the left and on down the steps, with a good view of the huge ditch. Turn half left at the bottom of the steps, heading for the gravel path which contours right along the hillside. This is a later 19th century railway. [Alternatively, to shorten the walk, head down the hill towards the lower stone bridge, joining the road]. *Continue along the upper contoured track, following the base of the Verne's rampart, around the corner, through a new bridge which carries a road over the path.* Just beyond (G) is the top of the incline for the Merchant's Railway, constructed in 1826. The trucks were dragged here by horses (locomotives had not yet been invented) and descended this steep slope by gravity alone, the empty trucks being sent back up by the weight of the full ones coming down.

Superb view of Portland Harbour from this point. *Return through the new bridge, but beyond the grassy patch don't go uphill to the path we used coming, but keep following the lower contoured path, which passes through apparently impenetrable scrub for parts of its route.* This is the line of the Merchant's Railway.

At the back of the housing estate the path meets a small road [and the short-cut rejoins the route]. Just beyond, take the path leading gently uphill to the left (H), another part of the Merchant's Railway, keep on along this path. The complex of cuttings and bridges on the slopes above are part of the series of later 19th century railways sending stone to the incline. Views of Chesil Bank and the Fleet behind open up. The path becomes a small road, with a few houses. The Old Rectory was here before the railway, since it partly dates from the 18th century. Just beyond the Old Rectory is a footpath called Old Hill, in fact the original main road up the fierce hill.

Follow the tarmac road uphill and take the path on the right to the main road. Cross, go left for 50 yards and then right, and right again and take grassy track (I) towards the cliff edge and to the stone seat. This is perhaps the best view on Portland, with the Harbour spread out on one side, and Chesil Bank in front. The Verne is particularly impressive from here.

West Weare, the tumbling undercliff below, was used for the dumping of overburden, and also has a huge landslip of 1859, caused by dumping too much waste on the cliff. 25 acres of land fell. The bedding of the stone is clear in the cliffs. We shall walk south along the cliff path.

Tout Quarries inland were worked extensively from the middle of the 19th century, and are now a sculpture quarry, where students come to make constructions with, or sculpt, the rock. Some are cut directly into the rock faces, some are free-standing while others are built of small fragments.

At the cliff walk level is a startling 1930s armchair of stone, and up the steps on the higher level a row of standing stones ornamented with drilled lines like those produced by the quarrying process and seen in quarried blocks all over the island. Close by are steps in the form of a snake. Explore the quarry to find dozens more. (Information boards).

Return to the cliff path and continue south. Tout Quarries had particularly complex internal railways, with some at a higher level needing bridges to carry them over the lower ones. Places where the overburden was tipped from trucks can be seen on the cliff edge and the bases of two bridges which spanned the path.

At the south end of the quarry, where the view opens up, take the path which branches left away from the cliff edge, towards a working quarry. Walk up the track towards the classical tower of St George's church. The track leads through dumps of stone and overburden. The big older buildings on the left were used for the stone trade.

The track joins the quarry road and emerges by the church (J). Huge graveyard, very bleak and full of Portland Stone gravestones, with the purple flowers of gladioli in May. St George's was finished in 1766, and is an unusual classical church, looking rather like a house. The early 19th century fittings inside are worth seeing (now redundant, usually open afternoons in summer). The church was paid for from the duty paid on stone exported from the island – the money was used for many communal projects like well-cleaning, looking after the weares or dumping grounds and so on.

Straight over the main road and down a track, turn right at the overgrown quarry, left along path at the back of the houses, taking right turn before the allotments along an alley through the houses to the main road (Reforne).

St George Reforne, Portland

Like most of the Portland villages, Reforne has plain small two or three storey houses of Portland Stone, many of them built from large blocks. Some are rendered, concealing the stone. Apsley House, a little way along, is dated 1815.

Left a little way along the road, cross over and turn right into Station Road (K). The station was replaced by brick houses in the 1970s. *Take the path marked NO CYCLING, and continue straight on, after 50 yards turn half left into a sunken garden, which was part of the railway line. Continue through the garden, across a road and between Portland Health Centre on the left and a school on the right. The path becomes a road, with a disused railway bridge on the left. At the end of the houses turn right into the gravel path which is heading for a circular stone building, the remains of a windmill* (L). *Keep heading towards the windmill.*

Portland has no rivers, so there were no water-mills. Two windmills are shown on a map of 1710, and both still survive here (although without their sails). They were used to grind corn until the late 19th century, and are the only surviving windmills in Dorset.

Turn left, heading towards the other windmill. The fields here were medieval strip fields until recently. Keep on along the track passing the windmill and a new deep quarry on the right. Go through the metal gate and turn right at the cross-roads of tracks. Both sides of the track are lined with huge lumps of recently quarried stone with letters and numbers on them giving their volume and type of stone. The quarry is on the right.

Keep along the track which joins the quarry road, and then on to the main road. Opposite is the finest house on Portland – Pennsylvania Castle, a marine villa of 1800, built by John Penn, the nephew of the founder of Pennsylvania. Penn diverted the road inland to its present line to create the grounds around his house. George III visited Pennyslvania Castle often when he was spending the summers at Weymouth.

Turn left along the main road, and the car park where the walk started is on the left. If you did not visit Portland Museum at the start of the walk, do so now.

Studland – Clay Digging and the Heathland

A walk through part of the vast area of heathland preserved at Studland, visiting the famous Agglestone, and reaching the shores of Poole Harbour at one of the very few points where this is possible. The whole walk is very good for seeing birds, and the heathland has many of the specialised plants which flourish in acid conditions. Huge views from the Agglestone, and very different, more intimate ones on the edge of Poole Harbour. Part of the route has to go through planted conifers, but the lighter natural woodland towards the harbour is more interesting.

The paths are well-marked and mostly dry off the heathland. Boggy patches on the heath can be very wet. The full walk is 9 miles (12½km) with 500ft (150m) of climbing. A short cut offers a medium length heathland walk of 5 miles (8km), and a yet shorter route is also possible.

Introduction: The heathlands are founded on mixed deposits of clay, sand and gravel, some in only small pockets, others much larger. The whole area has small pits produced by extraction of all these materials, but the most important and valuable deposit is china clay, which has been quarried since the 17th century for clay pipes and china making. From the 1770s the area supplied Josiah Wedgewood with the fine white clay which was a vital part of his famous 'Queen's Ware'. Many other Staffordshire firms bought clay from here, and extraction continues on a huge scale a little to the west.

The earliest railway in Dorset, running from one of the Norden (Corfe) pits to Poole Harbour, was built in 1806, using horses for motive power. Several other lines followed, we shall see part of the course of the longest one. These later lines were powered by steam engine.

Parking and Public Transport: The walk starts from Knoll Beach Car Park (A on the map) which belongs to the National Trust and charges non-members a fee. The car park is to the north of Studland village, off the Studland-Sandbanks road. In winter it might be possible to park on the road close by. Regular buses from Bournemouth, Poole and Swanage stop at the Knoll House Hotel – some open-topped in summer.

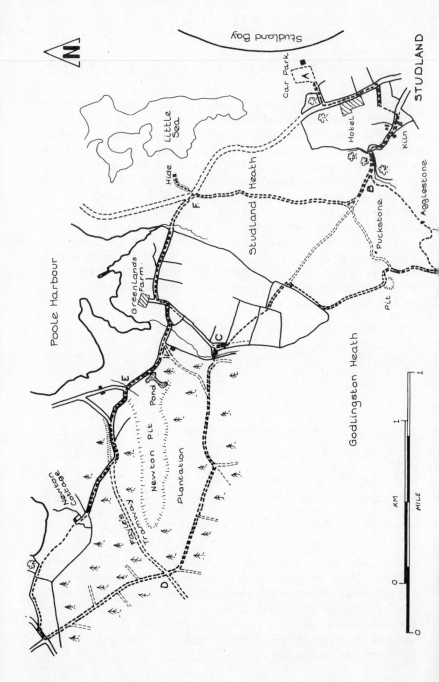

Information: Cafe, lavatories, information and shop at Knoll Beach Visitor Centre, open daily. More cafes, hotels and pubs in Studland village. Wildlife Information Centre at Little Sea open 12 noon to 6 p.m. Sundays and Bank Holidays.

Directions:
Walk back up the road which leads into the car park, and turn left along the main road, along past the Knoll House Hotel. After 400 yds (365m), turn right through a blue gate signed Bridleway. Keep straight ahead along this path until it reaches open ground. Turn half left across this open area, heading under the power lines for a post visible in the gap in the hedge. The Agglestone is clearly seen in the distance on the right from the middle of the open patch.

Turn right along the gravel track. The brick structure a little way up on the left is the remains of a brick kiln which operated around 1900. *Keep on along the track straight ahead (signposted Agglestone), ignoring a left turn.* Heathstone and brick cottages to the right. The light woodland, with birches mixed with a variety of other trees is typical of these poor soils. *Keep on along the track, through the gate, crossing the stream on a little bridge, and then bearing left. We emerge into open heathland, and 50 yards on take the path to the left (B). This goes up and down small hills towards the Agglestone.* This huge area of heathland is preserved as a Nature Reserve. All six native species of reptile live here – grass snakes, vipers, common lizard, slow worm, smooth snakes and sand lizards. The last two are very rare, but flourish here. Many rare birds are also found, including the Dartford Warbler. The vegetation is dominated by heather and furze, but uncommon orchids and gentians are to be found, and the insect-eating sundews in boggy areas. *Keep on along the path until the Agglestone is reached.* Don't look back until you have climbed right up to the Agglestone.

The Agglestone views are wide. In clear weather the Isle of Wight is visible to the right, and the sea is always seen. Straight ahead are the white buildings of Sandbanks, over the mouth of the harbour. The cliffs of Bournemouth are beyond. To the left Poole harbour stretches a surprising distance inland, with Poole itself just visible.

The Agglestone itself is a large lump of gritstone, vividly coloured. It used to sit on a smaller base, but collapsed down a bit in 1970. The Victorians thought it must have been a huge Druid's altar – but it is totally natural. Folklore says the Devil threw it from the Isle of Wight.

Leave the Agglestone by the path opposite the one we came up by. Turn right after 50 yards to take another clear path which

The Agglestone

*contours around the next knoll. The path meets a sandy track – turn
sharp right along the track and keep on along here, turning left at
the first junction.* The depression on the left, just beyond a lone pine
tree, is an old clay pit. The clay deposits are spread all over a wide
area, so the pits are not concentrated at one point. They are very
difficult to date – this one is shown disused on a map of 1888. *Keep
on along the track until it meets a wire fence, turn right continuing
along the track until it meets a major path.* [The really short walk
turns right along this path which leads back to the path we entered
the heath by, and back to the car park up the road]. *The main route
turns left, through a boggy part and two wicket gates, then straight
ahead along a grassy path through gorse towards the conifer plantations. Go through the gate straight ahead into a field, heading
towards another gate a little way along the right hand fence. Go
through that gate, and diagonally across the field to a gate in the far
corner.*

The pasture fields have been reclaimed from the heathland this
century. Converting heath to farmland was common from the 17th
century, but now heathlands are largely destroyed by afforestation

or urban development.

Go through the gate and on straight ahead for 100 yards along the grassy path [the medium length walk continues straight ahead along a path through fields which becomes a track and rejoins the longer walk just before the entrance to Greenlands Farm].

The main route turns left (signed Rempstone) by a wooden shed, (C), into woodland, across a stream on stepping stones and through a wicket gate into conifers. Turn right up the gravel track, and keep straight on along it. 100 yards along on the right the humps of clay dumps can be seen in the trees.

Until 1950 heathland stretched from Ridge near Wareham to Studland, broken only by small settlements and clay pits, but between 1950-1954, 1,500 acres of conifers were planted by the Forestry Commission.

Ignore a right turn, but when the track reaches a T-junction, turn right. Keep on along the track, ignoring a left turn. Turn right at the next junction, and immediately through by a barrier to a minor tarmac road (D). The road is on the line of the longest of the clay railways, built in 1905 from the pits at Norden near Corfe for five miles to Goathorn Point where the clay was transferred to ships. The line across the heathland was lifted in the Second World War. Parts were used until 1969, but most of its route was taken over and improved as one of the roads used by the oil extraction companies. The route here is a slight cutting – railways had to have very gentle slopes. It was usually called either Fayle's Tramway (after the name of the firm) or the Goathorn Railway. We shall rejoin its route later on.

Go straight over the road up the track opposite, past a barrier. We are still in conifers. *Keep on along the sandy track ignoring turns to right and left. The sandy track emerges from the conifers into a small field. Cross the field on the track, and then turn right at the junction, up a gravel road, slightly uphill. At the top of the hill (after only about 100 yards) turn right through a field gate (waymarked) and take the track running straight ahead across the fields.* Ower Farm can be seen on the left. *Keep on the track, which turns right. Go through a gate in the corner of the field leading to a track be-tween a wood on the left and a shrubby bank.* The field on the right is one of the sites suggested for Newton, a new town founded in 1286, which failed soon afterwards.

Good view over the inlet of Poole Harbour as the track (now becoming a path) leaves the wood. Furzey Island is straight ahead at the end of the inlet. Many water birds. Ower was a centre for salt production from the 11th century through medieval times. Salt water was evaporated in pans along the shore.

Keep on along the path to Newton Cottage, but look back just before reaching it to see a large view of Poole Harbour. Go through the gate by the cottage, along the drive, through another gate and on up the hill beyond on the gravel road. The natural pine woodlands on the left contrast with the planted conifers on the right. At the junction with the tarmac road, look right – this is the road on the 1905 railway route which we crossed earlier. To the right of the road was a second line which led through clay washing beds, now completely covered in conifers. The iron gate on our left was perhaps contemporary with the railway, and the flat area beyond is part of the line. *Turn left along the tarmac road.* The railway route runs parallel to the left, mostly in a shallow cutting. *Keep on along the tarmac road. Where this road turns to the left (and is marked private) we go straight on along the gravel track.* The railway continued on roughly the line of the tarmac road, up the now inaccessible Goathorn peninsula to a jetty on Poole Harbour.

Keep on along the gravel track. The Victorian brick buildings just visible on the left were part of another railway, only a mile long, running from the pits to our right, the Newton pits, to Goathorn peninsula and built in 1868. *Keep on along the gravel track, and stop at the next junction* (E). To the left, in the angle of the two roads, a row of six cottages for the clay workers was built, with another two on the other side of the road, all now completely gone. *Turn right along the gravel road crossing the stream on a low concrete bridge,* originally used by both road and rail. *Keep on along the gravel road, ignoring a left turn.* A gap in the hedge on the left, by some old pine trees, marks the entrance to the area where Newton School was built. Nothing remains of the building, which was also used for church services. After it closed as a school in the 1920s the children were taken to school at Corfe in a passenger carriage on the clay railway. The Newton pits declined in the 1930s and were abandoned in 1939.

A little way along on the right a big pond can be seen, part of the huge Newton claypits. The dumps we saw when walking through the conifer plantation are on the other side of these pits, which extend for more than 1000 yds (1km) westwards. *Keep on along the gravel road, ignoring right turns.* After the road crosses a little creek, there is a short uphill part. Almost at the top of the hill, set in the middle of the road are 8ft (2.5m) lengths of iron rail from one of the clay railways, and just beyond are some of the small iron 'shoes' which held the rails on the sleepers. All these must have been brought from Newton as the railways never extended in this direction.

Keep on along the gravel track, which turns to the left soon after the top of the hill [medium route rejoins here]. Then follow the track right at the entrance to Greenlands Farm. We are wriggling along the edge of Poole Harbour, with occasional glimpses of the water. *The road emerges into open heathland and then meets the public road to Sandbanks ferry* (F). A short excursion off the main route to the Wildlife Information Centre is well worth while (open Suns and Bank Holidays). *Take the sunken path indicated on the opposite side of the road to reach the hide with its wonderful views over Little Sea.* Lots of birds including waders, gulls and over-wintering wildfowl.

Retrace your steps back to the road, cross over, and go through the gate opposite by the English Nature signboard onto a track leading southwards across the open heathland. After 50 yards we join another track and bear left (signpost 'English Nature Permitted Bridleway'). Keep on along this track and from the top of the first rise, the Agglestone is visible straight ahead: the track snakes towards it. *Just over the second rise, take the left hand track where it forks, heading towards Studland village. Take the next left downhill towards the woods. Ignore minor paths to the right which lead towards the Agglestone.* The track here is deeply rutted. Just before the woods by a wooden signpost we rejoin our outward route to take the same paths back to car park (B). *Keep on the track through the wood, over the bridge on the stream, on uphill past the cottages and through a gate. Turn left through a gateway just before the brow of the hill and head across the open field towards a solitary oak.* Good view of Bournemouth in the distance to the right. *Turn right at the oak tree along a wide grassy hedged path to the main road. Turn left along the road to reach the car park.*

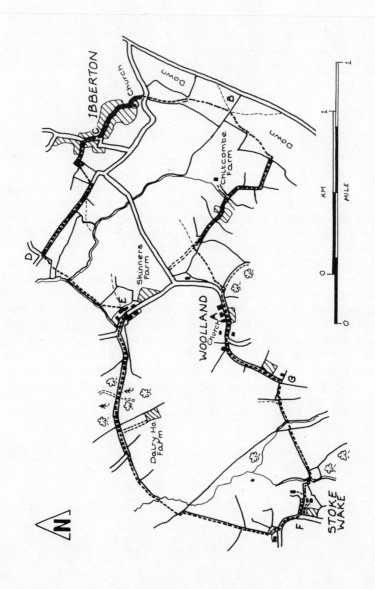

Woolland – the Victorian Estate

A walk around Woolland and into Ibberton and Stoke Wake, taking the easiest way up the steep chalk scarp overlooking the Blackmore Vale. Inevitably the ascent of the scarp is a pretty stiff climb, but it is worth it for the views. Some of the paths are waymarked, and all are easy to find. Down off the chalk, the paths can be muddy and even difficult if it is really wet. The whole walk is 5 miles (8½km) with 650ft (195m) of climbing, but a short cut offers a walk of 3 miles (5km).

Introduction: An 1849 catalogue for the sale of the 'very valuable and complete Domain comprising (with the exception of only about 14 acres) the Entire Parish of Woolland' gives much detail of the area in early Victorian times, and emphasises the 'highly Picturesque, Boldly Undulated, Richly Timbered' landscape. The purchaser was being offered an estate sufficiently complete to make him a gentleman: 1,100 acres divided into four farms, then all tenanted, provided income; the mansion a suitable country residence with ornamental grounds, and the woods for sport – 'woodlands and covers peculiarly suited for the preservation of game'. The parish was greatly 'improved' by the purchaser, and we shall explore his domain, as well as venturing onto his neighbours' land. The churches of the three parishes show the variety of Victorian 'restoration'.

Parking: Drive to Woolland village (7 miles, 11km) west of Blandford, in a maze of very pretty minor roads but well signposted. Park on the wide part of the road by the church (A on the map ST 776069), being careful not to obstruct the road. There is no public transport available.

Directions:
Walk up the path to the church, which was 'restored' by being totally rebuilt in 1855. The 1849 catalogue claimed that the church did not come under the Bishop's jurisdiction, but in order to have the new church consecrated, the owner had to admit that it did. In the left hand side of the porch are built-in collecting boxes 'For the Poor' and 'County Hospital' – very Victorian. Inside the apse is very pretty, with lots of different coloured marbles, and deeply carved capitals showing local plants. The bills for the carving survive –

capitals cost £1.25p each, small bosses 12½p. A brass at the back of the church is to the memory of Montague Williams, the land-owner and builder of the church.

Return to the road – the stone cottage opposite is Victorian, and once was the school. *Turn left along the road.* The Clock turret is on the stables of the big house, now themselves converted to a dwelling. The big house was destroyed by fire this century. *200 yards along from the church turn right and then immediately left through a Victorian kissing gate in iron railings.* We shall see many of these expensive gates round Woolland. *Keep straight ahead on the faint path, branching right after 50 yards (signposted Ibberton) and follow the waymarked posts across the field downhill.* This pasture is being taken over by tiny trees, and more have been planted on the far side. The house visible to the left was part of the 14 acres not for sale in 1849.

When we reach the overgrown hedge we cross the stream on a bridge and keep straight on and soon reach a waymarked post on a tarmac road. Turn right up this road. Good view of the chalk scarp. *Keep on along the road, passing a bungalow and then very plain Victorian cottages with farm buildings to match.* These were built after 1849, and are now stables. *Keep on the road, down a little hill, over a stream, taking the second right at the junction just beyond.* The track is signed 'Turnworth Road ¾'. Look through the gap to the left a little way up to see Chitcombe Farm, described in 1848 as 'an excellent newly built farmhouse and all requisite farm buildings'. In medieval times there was a separate hamlet here. *Continue up the track (rightish), which is a deep hollow way here, with old hazel each side, and lots of ferns and moss. Where several field entrances meet, the lane we need is clearly marked Bridleway, half left. The lane becomes a path* and the underlying Greensand shows clearly in the old badgers' sets. This part (up the 'bold undulation' of 1849) is steep, but think of the views from the top. *Turn left at the top into overgrown scrub and then out into downland which is now also rather overgrown, with mostly long grass. Keep on the path heading diagonally uphill.* In 1849 all these upper parts were open downland grazed by sheep. A huge view opens up – with Woolland directly below us and the Blackmore Vale and Somerset beyond. Below are the stables we walked through, looking tiny now. In 1849 Woolland was described as having 'a large proportion of *Superior Grass Land*, and some *Ornamental Plantations and Woods*, thickly stored with *Thriving Oak, Larch etc.*, and abounding with *Fine Elm and Hedge-Row Timber*'. The elms have all died, but the rest still fits – the hedges are still thickly wooded, there are even more

Woolland village

plantations of trees and still much pasture.

Continue along the path, which wriggles through scrub, and then along with the hedge on our left. Through more scrub to meet an overgrown hedge with tall trees (B). This is the parish boundary, and going through the gate we leave Woolland and enter Ibberton. Good view, with Duntish Hill straight ahead and Alfred's Tower visible to the left, at the end of the ridge. The downland here is open, but the grass has been 'improved'. *Walk downhill across the field ahead on the broad 'shelf' heading for a break in far hedge to the right of a double electricity pole. Go through the break in the hedge, and keep on downhill with the hedge on your left. This path becomes a track: keep on down it to the gate at the bottom corner. Go through the gate and across the tarmac road to a gravel track signposted 'Halter Path to Ibberton'.* Presumably halter is a variant of bridle path. *Ignore path to the right and continue down the track.* Odd turnstile gate by the church which appears on the left, set on shelf in the hillside. Ibberton church is a great contrast to Woolland – instead of being demolished, the late medieval church was properly restored in 1903, although it had got into an appalling state (see photograph inside church). Even so, this thoughtful restoration abolished many simple old fittings.

Go back to the track and continue downhill and through to the village. Ibberton village is also different from Woolland – Ibberton is larger, has more of a centre and houses and cottages in a medley of styles and dates. It was not an estate village – and did not have a single big landowner like Woolland. If it had, the church would probably have been rebuilt in the middle of the 19th century. There are still farms in the middle of the little village. Just before the road junction is the Crown pub, usefully placed for refreshment.

At the junction (C) turn right by a charmingly prim brick and thatch cottage of about 1800 *and walk along the road for about* 150 *yards and turn left down a gravelly road between a thatched cottage and farmhouse. Keep on along this track, which changes to concrete and then gravel. At the end turn left through a gate beyond the farm buildings and go straight across the field to a gate by a shed. Through the gate and turn right down a muddy lane which seems to have a little stream running along it. Keep on down this lane with its high hedges each side, ignoring a waymarked footpath to the left and several field entrances. When the track turns right, immediately after a gate (D) turn left through a gate (waymarked) and go straight ahead with the hedge on your left for a short distance, and then cut across the field to a stile. Continue straight across the next field, over another stile, straight on across the field beyond heading to the left of an isolated oak.* Good views of the chalk scarp to the left, including the bit we walked, which is clearly visible because of the change in vegetation each side of the parish boundary.

Go over the stile and footbridge and on straight ahead with the ditch then a hedge on our right to another stile by a cattle trough, over stile and then turn half left towards a path between the pair of brick houses to emerge at a tarmac road (E). There are more houses here now than in the 'centre' of Woolland, and that was also true in 1848. Parts of the 14 acres not for sale were here, along with five cottages and a farm.

[The shortened route turns left here, and proceeds along the road back to Woolland. Ignore turning to the left]. *The main route turns right up the road, and then left at the junction (signposted Hazelbury Bryan, Kings Stag). Keep on along the road, which passes through one of the woods shown on the* 1848 *map.* Halfway through the woods, on either side of the road are expensive iron gates, part of a Victorian carriage drive. This wood bordered the 'tastefully laid out' pleasure grounds around the house, which in 1849 were 'embellished with a variety of foreign and native shrubs'. The wood has some ornamental pines and exotic trees, as well as traditional oaks, under-planted with hazel. The road widens as we leave the wood, and also has fine oaks. To the left is Dairy House Farm, one of the 'Four Excellent Farms' offered in 1848. It is still a dairy farm.

When the road turns right, keep straight on through a gate into a field, and on along the hedge past the zig-zag in our hedge on the left, to the far corner. Cross the small stream (it is narrower a little bit downstream) and go straight over the field ahead, between the two oak trees to reach the gate beyond. Go through the gate, left to the corner of the field and then right uphill, keeping the hedge on the left (the route may be altered to go over the sleeper bridge and up the other side of the hedge – follow the waymarkers and keep uphill). Keep on up here, through a gate and on straight ahead up the side of the field. The two cottages straight ahead are part of Stoke Wake which barely seems a hamlet now, but in 1861, 67 men and 56 women agricultural labourers lived here, besides the gentry.

Go left through the gate at the top and straight ahead uphill to the tarmac road. Turn left along the road, and left again at the first driveway (Marked footpath) 200 yards along (F) (for a house called 'Another Old Rectory'). 100 yards down, just before the sharp bend left in the drive (by a footpath marker), turn right into trees to reach a waymarked wicket gate. Go through the gate, and Stoke Wake church (now redundant) is straight ahead. It was rebuilt in 1872 in a much simpler and cheaper style than Woolland church. Stoke Wake also had a tiny school at the head of the Rectory drive. *Turn sharp left immediately inside the gate, and follow the fence, down steps and on along the hedge just inside the garden and orchard. Towards the bottom turn right across the orchard to reach a stile and bridge. Go over, and head for a stile (not the gate) opposite. Cross the stile and a concrete bridge (one hand rail broken off) and go uphill to soon join a track. Right uphill along the track to a wicket gate, then left uphill once through the gate. Walk along the edge of the field, with the hedge on your left. Go over the stile at the corner into woodland, downhill and then across a tiny stream and through a metal kissing gate into a field.* The metal gate is another Victorian one and marks the Woolland boundary. *Keep straight ahead uphill and then down, with the hedge on your left. Through another kissing gate and then towards cottages (G). When you reach the gravel road turn left.* Hill Farm a little way along, was built after the 1848 map and before 1887, and is a good example of a purpose-built farm, with a very solid stone farmhouse and large neat brick farm buildings. A few small later buildings have been added. *Keep on along the gravel road.* On the left at the end of the road is Ivy Cottage, shown on the 1848 map as a Keepers' Cottage.

Turn left along the tarmac road. The Keeper's Cottage on the right was built in the 1870s or 80s in chunky stone like Hill Farm. Victorian iron railings on the right. The old stone house on the right just before the church was the farmhouse for Hill Farm in 1848 – it was the Manor House in the 17th century. The car is parked by the church.

Bovington – Tanks in the Heathland

A walk through heathland and the Frome valley, with a surprising amount of woodland. Lawrence of Arabia's cottage (Cloud's Hill) and grave are on the route, as is Moreton church with its fabulous glass, and natural features like Culpepper's Dish, a huge solution-hole, and Rimsmoor Pond. Deer live in the woodlands, and many birds. The paths are well-marked and there is hardly any climbing (350 feet (105m) over the whole walk). The complete route is 6 miles (10km), but a short cut offers a 3 mile (5km) walk.

Introduction: Dorset's heathlands were created by woodland clearance in prehistoric times. On acidic soils the vegetation became dominated by heather, producing the heaths. In the mid-18th century Dorset had 40,000 hectares (nearly 100,000 acres) of heathland, but reclamation for agriculture and urban development has reduced the area to less than an eighth of the 18th century figure. The heaths were regarded as barren wasteland, cheap land suitable for army camps like Bovington. 1,000 acres were purchased here for the Army in 1899, for a rifle range and tented camp. Tanks were invented in the First World War, and the Tank Training Centre moved to Bovington in 1916 because the heaths were like the part of France then being fought over. Bovington remains the home of the Royal Tank Corps.

This southern Dorset heathland is the setting for Thomas Hardy's novel *The Return of the Native*, (1878): he describes all its moods and changes and the struggles of its few inhabitants.

Parking and Public Transport: Drive to Bovington, and take the road north towards Cloud's Hill. About ½ mile (1km) from the edge of the built-up area on the right is a car park by a 'Tanks Crossing' sign (A). Park here. Buses run fairly frequently from Wool Railway Station to Bovington Camp, and there are occasional buses from Dorchester to Cloud's Hill.

Information: Lawrence's Cottage (Cloud's Hill) (fee) belongs to the National Trust and is open Wed, Thurs, Fri, Suns and bank holiday Mondays 2-5pm, May-October. The Tank Museum (fee) is open daily 10am – 5pm except Christmas (01929 405096).

The vast Tank Training ground by the car park partially preserves a great swathe of heathland, and has a notice board

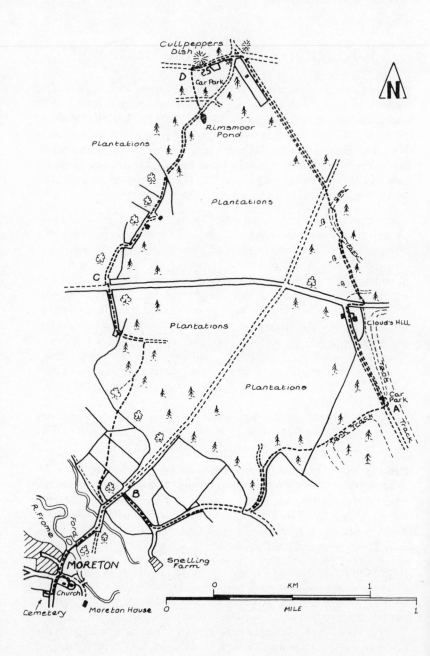

Cullpeppers Dish

D   Car Park

Rimsmoor Pond

Plantations

Plantations

TRACK

C

Cloud's Hill

Plantations

Car Park

A   TRACK

Plantations

Plantations

Fast Track

B

Snelling Farm

R. Frome

Ford

MORETON

Church

Cemetery   Moreton House

KM   0 ——————— 1

MILE   0 ——————— 1

N

explaining the great variety of tanks which may go by. A complete series of tanks from the First World War onwards can be seen in the Tank Museum at Bovington: visit it after the walk.

The small oak tree planted by the roadside in the car park is a memorial to T.E. Lawrence who crashed his motorbike close to this spot in 1935 and died in Bovington Camp hospital a few days later.

Directions:

Cross over the road, and go left for 20 yards, then right to the footpath marked through an area used by tanks and showing much bare gravel. Go over the stile and straight down the footpath. A good sample of natural heathland to the right, with heather and some pines, contrasting with the serried ranks of conifers planted on the left.

Tanks were top secret when first invented: roads were closed for traffic when they moved to Bovington, and one Dorset shepherd who in 1916 refused to leave his flock was enclosed in hurdles by the Army to prevent his seeing the new device passing by. A local farmer complained that he didn't mind being kept away from the new secret weapon, but would the Army please remove the broken-down one which had been towed into his farmyard and left there for two days.

Keep on along the path until it separates from the tank track, and after 100 yards the footpath turns right over a stile into coniferous woods. Keep on downhill, with rhododendrons lining the path. At the bottom of the hill the path joins a track. Turn left along the track. Keep on along here, through a gap by a gate and then turn right along another track. More open heathland along here, sandy, with some oak and birch. The track is still wooded, but now with fields either side. The double bank on the left is part of the water-supply system for water meadows, which were formed very early here. The bridges along this part are early 19th century brick.

Continue along the track, bearing right at the entrance to 'Snelling Farm', to a T-junction (B), and turn left, continuing on this track, ignoring paths to left and right, to reach a river. Go over the bridge and then half right and keep along the track straight ahead. Look to the right just before the second river is reached to see a Second World War pillbox of concrete and brick in the hedge. Lines of these were defences against tanks, ironic since tank drivers had trained in this area since 1916.

The path reaches the second river – the River Frome, which is wide and picturesque here. Cross on the long footbridge, and keep on up the road past the shop, looking to the right along the road by the shop to see the typical heathland village cottages, with cob walls set on stone footings. Several are still thatched.

Go left soon afterwards through the white gate, along the road to Moreton House and the church. Turn right up to the church, which is a fanciful Gothic revival building of 1776 and the 1840s. Go inside to see the unique engraved glass in all the windows, created by Laurence Whistler from 1955. The window in the chapel to the right is a memorial to a pilot who died in the Second World War. The fine effigy of T.E. Lawrence is in St Martins, Wareham (see Walk 5) having been refused by Moreton church.

Moreton Church

Retrace your steps back to the road (right out of church, left down the drive) and turn left and straight on at the main road, to the cemetery which is on the right. T.E. Lawrence's grave is at the far end, large and well-lettered. He died over 60 years ago, but floral tributes are regularly placed on the grave.

Turn left on leaving the cemetery retracing your steps along the road back to the wide River Frome, over the footbridge and along the gravel track back to the other river. [For the shorter route, continue along the track ahead (the one we came in on), ignoring all right and left turns and after about 1 mile you reach a tarmac road.

Turn right to reach Lawrence of Arabia's cottage]. *50 yards beyond the river on the track we came by, turn left over a stile with 'Jubilee Trail' waymarked.* We shall follow these waymarkers to the next road, a great help through the woods. (Trail created to celebrate 60 years of the Ramblers Association, 1995: full trail runs 90 miles across all Dorset). *Walk diagonally to the right across the field to the corner of the woodland, and then along the fence to the stile by the water trough. Go over the stile, and on diagonally left across the next field, over another stile, across the corner of a field to yet another stile (a double one with a plank bridge over a ditch) and on straight ahead to a stile into the woods.* The outer part of the wood is broadleaf trees. Scotch Firs were planted in the Moreton area from the middle of the 18th century and this century heathlands everywhere have been used for conifer plantations by the Forestry Commission. *Follow the Jubilee Trail markers through the wood: take the clear path leading ahead, turning right where the markers indicate at the T-junction of paths, and then left at the next track. Keep on along this track, past a barrier blocking it, and turn right when open fields are reached, and straight on along the fenced path. At the public road (C) go straight over and up a metaled track with a finger post 'Culpepper's Dish'. Continue up the track which zig-zags through oak woodland. Just after you pass a cottage on the right, the path diverges from the track, leading straight ahead. Keep on along here and follow a Jubilee Trail waymarker where it indicates a right turn towards the top of the hill, and you are soon into open heathland with conifers.*

Go along the wide gravel path uphill straight ahead for 500 yards and on the right is a boggy pond called Rimsmoor. Peat has formed in the hollow here for more than 8,000 years, and is almost 60 feet (18m) deep at one point. The pollen preserved in a core taken from this pond in the 1980s gives a complete vegetational history of the area.

Take the path waymarked to the left just after the pond, passing through bracken and pines. Cross a gravel track and continue on the path, up a short steep hill to a gravel track just before a tarmac road (D). Turn right to reach a car park, which has a good view back across the heathland valley. *Cross the tarmac road,* opposite the entrance to car park, to look down into Culpepper's Dish, the largest and deepest of the many solution hollows in this area. It is 250 feet (80m) across and 66 feet (20m) deep. These solution holes are formed where gravel or other acidic deposits overlie the chalk: the weak acid formed eats the chalk away at certain points and produces these hollows.

Walk down the tarmac road (right with your back to the car park), past the discreet water reservoir and a smaller 'dish' on the right. At the cross roads take the right turn signed 'Bovington'. Keep on along this road which has good wild flowers in the verges, to the next junction. Go straight over the road at the junction and on to the waymarked path through piney heathland, cross over a track used by tanks and continue along our track, which runs alongside and then re-joins the tank track. Soon afterwards, by a tree with a painted blue flash, turn right onto a track which runs through fairly open heathland. The area to the right had trenches like those of the First World War battlefields constructed in it from 1916 for the tanks to practise in. *Keep on by the electricity cables, ignoring a path to the right. When the track reaches a junction at the bottom of a steep hill, keep straight on up the steep hill and on along the track a short distance to the gap in the fence, and down to the main road. Cross over the road, and turn right (downhill) to the junction and then left a little way to Cloud's Hill, Lawrence's Cottage, (National Trust).*

After his huge successes in Arabia in the First World War, Colonel T.E. Lawrence bizarrely re-enlisted in 1923 as a simple soldier and was posted to Bovington. He rented and then bought this tiny gamekeeper's cottage, using it as a refuge from the Army Camp. He fitted it out ready for his retirement in 1935, but died only a few weeks later. Well worth seeing inside. Lawrence described the cottage and the heath as 'very quiet, very lonely, very bare'.

Turn left on leaving the cottage, and the car is parked a little way down the road. The area on the left was full of redundant tanks left over from the First World War when Lawrence lived here. Drive into Bovington to visit the tank museum.